Voice For The Silent Fathers

EDDIE K. WRIGHT

Eddie K. Wright

VOICE FOR THE SILENT FATHERS

ACKNOWLEDGMENTS

I want to thank my immediate family and my family from the B.O.P. who's support and enthusiasm to write about this taboo topic was essential to its completion. James W. Davenport (Twin), my first jailhouse editor and critic, George Sepulveda, (Paradise), Rasheed Holmes, Javier Colon and Sony Sanchez who were all always on call for my reading sessions in cell #118. To my cell mates throughout the years who put up with my late night writing exploits.

A special acknowledgment to Scott Niemic, writing coach and re-visioning extraordinaire. To Rita Lane my copyeditor, thanks for your insight and positive feedback. To Diane Yuskin, my line editor, thank you for your thoroughness and attention to detail. To Amber Colbert for the insightful forward, Gail Holmes for the penetrating back cover quote and to Shirl Tyner, for the amazing book cover design.

Finally, to Mimi, my sister and CEO of M Wright Group, LLC who allowed me to sit in the passenger seat once she took control of this project, finding ways to get the exposure needed with me being in the confines of a maximum federal penitentiary. The limited phone minutes and lock downs, along with all the other unexpected issues never prevented her from finding some creative way to get the job done. I send my thanks, gratitude and love to you all.

Eddie K. Wright, AKA Gangster turned Guru.

FOREWARD

I remember my first time meeting Eddie. I was an undergrad living in Los Angeles and like every young Angelino, I was fascinated by the entertainment world, celebrities and Hollywood. I got a call from my sister-from-another-mister Mimi, that her brother Eddie was in town with Erick Sermon and wanted to know if we wanted to go to one of his shows. It was finally happening – after all the stories I heard about Eddie, I was finally going to get a taste of his celebrity lifestyle. After screaming, jumping, up and down, running around my dorm room for what felt like a solid 10 minutes, I started planning what outfit would best compliment my blonde braids.

Everything about Eddie was just... cool. There's really no other word for it. When he met us at the backstage door and gave us our passes, he had a calm demeanor and a charismatic smile that let you know he was in control. As I walked through the backstage area, passing hip hop legends like Ice Cube, Chuck D of Public Enemy, on our way to meeting Erick Sermon (and my personal favorite) Redman, I remember thinking *Don't embarrass yourself. Don't embarrass Mimi. And definitely don't embarrass Eddie! Just stay calm or you'll never be invited to anything ever again!* To say Eddie seemed comfortable, that he had swag, that he was confident, just doesn't paint the full picture. While he was not an artist in the forefront on stage, it seemed like he knew the real power of being behind the stage and unlike me, he wasn't just along for the ride, but he was navigating the waters of the hip-hop industry.

Before meeting Profit, Eddie's better known alias at the time, for years I had heard stories from Mimi about her little brother Eddie – their adventures growing up in Long Island, giving their mother grief with their adolescent mischief, and about his young son Andrew. In fact, I also remember my first time meeting Andrew. He had to be about 8 years old. He came out to visit his cool Aunt Mimi (it runs in the family) in San Diego and she was taking him and her oldest son to the community pool. He had the same charismatic smile as his father, but also a light hearted and playful spirit.

1

Some may say that Eddie was living two different lives. But I don't believe that's an accurate depiction of Eddie's life or mindset at that time. It's not that Eddie was not himself in all areas of his life. All the stories I heard about him as a teenager, spending time with his son, mother, and sister, even hanging out with him backstage at other events (I was able to hold it together well enough to be invited out again), I saw a consistent image of Eddie. It was in reading Eddie's story, that it helped me to make sense of what Eddie was experiencing. I came to see a young father trying to balance all the aspects of his life. On one hand, he had the tough, street-wise world which requires a strong, unemotional, masculine stance and on the other, a young son who was coming into his own in a way Eddie could not understand and that contradicted the "manly" mentality he had come to construct. Through Voice for the Silent Fathers, we are privileged to go on this journey of understanding what it means to challenge a mindset of prejudice and preconceived notions and to build a relationship founded on love and acceptance.

While Voice for the Silent Fathers is a personal narrative, it speaks to a much larger issue. Often discussions about homosexuality tend to be one-dimensional narratives, lumping all experiences under the LGBTQ umbrella. Many of the stories about parents and accepting their gay children are often written by mothers, or from a son's perspective to his parent, and in nearly all of these accounts race is never discussed.

It is important to understand how race and gender play a role when it comes to discussing sexuality. In communities of color, especially the Black community, sexuality in general is not discussed in a family setting and homosexuality seems to be off limits. In Black families, there are heteronormative assumptions about a child – he's going to grow up, get married to a woman, and have children – end of story. Anything that strays outside of this life plan is either ignored on a passive end or met with hostility on a more aggressive end. It seems as though the attitude is much like Eddie describes – "No son of mine."

This supposed comfort of silence and turning a blind-eye is actually damaging to the African American community. There is a disconnected belief that by simply not discussing homosexuality, it will not be seen or felt by those who do not identify as gay. But this could not be further from the truth. In the early 2000's, there were discussions about the alarming rates of HIV infection among young, straight African American women, in committed relationships, many of them wives and girlfriends. Then J.L. King's On the Down Low let the secret out – Black men were secretly engaging in risky sex with other men and then transmitting sexual infections to their female partners. And while engaging in secretive sex is not a new phenomenon, what was new about the "down low" culture was how it was shaped by hypermasculine attitudes about Black male sexuality.

As a straight Black woman, I was very concerned about what I was reading. My graduate studies led me to research more about this problem to get to the root of the attitudes about gender and sexuality, specifically in the African American community. My findings echoed what others, like King, have concluded - that this "turn a blind eye", "no son of mine", macho-man attitude in the Black community leads many young men to feel like they have to hide their sexuality from their loved ones in fear of rejection. In hiding their sexuality, they then engage in risky behavior. But risky sexual behavior is just one of the outcomes of this "hush-hush" attitude surrounding homosexuality. Depression, physical violence, family rejection, drug use and suicide are all unfortunate and avoidable consequences of this secretive stance on homosexuality.

Eddie's journey is not only unique in that it discusses acceptance from a straight Black man's perspective, but it fills a huge void in the discussion on homosexuality. It is necessary, especially for Black men, because even though Eddie's story is personal, it is one that many men will be able to relate to. We can no longer bury our heads in the sand and pretend that homosexuality does not exist, or that it in no way connected to the lives of straight people. And even more importantly, we can no longer pretend that the silence and misunderstandings of straight fathers are not impacting their relationships with their children.

The stories Eddie shares in Voices for the Silent Fathers are honest, real, and raw. Eddie does not hold back on sharing his most intimate thoughts and emotions. It is important to keep in mind when reading Eddie's story that we've all been Eddie at some point in our lives when it comes to our relationships. When we don't understand something, fear arises in us, creating a number of responses. We try to ignore what we don't understand. Sometimes we try to run from what we don't understand. When we grow tired of running, we desperately try to change what we don't understand. All the while, we must come to the conclusion that Eddie has reached – that perfect love casts out fear. Eddie's story is one of learning to perfect the love that he has for his son by not being afraid of what he doesn't understand, but learning to work through his anxieties to a place of acceptance.

As a sociology professor, and one who advocates for public sociology I teach from an applied and public sociology standpoint and I often remind my students that they have an obligation to themselves, their families, and their communities to make use of the information presented in my courses for positive social change. Voice for the Silent Fathers is more than a story about a father's love for his son – it is a work of applied and public sociology. Eddie's brave vulnerability is ushering in a change to the way men, especially Black men, approach difficult subjects – with genuine and direct openness and sincerity. His story and struggles with fatherhood will not just touch those who are struggling with their child's sexuality – but are going through the process of learning what it means to love their child no matter what.

Amber Colbert, M.A.

INTRODUCTION

Was there anything I could do to stop my son's homosexuality? When did I know my son was gay? What made him that way? I've witnessed the desperation in the eyes of fathers, from all walks of life, who have pulled me aside, away from listening ears, wanting to know the answers to their questions, analyzing the possibilities of why their son might be gay, some weren't even sure that their sons were gay.

Mothers seem to be more liberal about their son's decisions to choose what makes them happy in life, and most importantly, "who" they share their lives with. However, for fathers, nine times out of ten, the topic is taboo. Especially the fathers who I've met in Federal prison or on the opposite end of the spectrum working with celebrities in the entertainment business.

I can tell you this though, I never thought I would write a book and never a book on a topic like this, but life is funny that way. I found myself raising a son at 18 years old; I was still a kid myself, with a baby boy headed down that taboo highway. I was confused, frustrated, and angry at the world. *"Why me?"* I often thought in those early days... "Why has life thrown me this crazy curve ball?"

Back then it wasn't so easy to talk to my friends about my son's odd behavior, some things you just didn't talk about it. So I struggled alone, doing everything I could to stop the unstoppable because I wanted a son who would grow to be a man like me. I wanted a son that had lots girlfriends and would one day save up three months' salary at his very manly job and place an engagement ring on the finger of the woman who stole his heart, his beautiful future wife, not some... "Life Partner."

Back then, with my limited knowledge of being gay, I would picture a pervert, infected with AIDS that molested little boys, because isn't that what homosexuals do? In the crowd I hung out with I wasn't the only person to think that way. If Drew chose that path, I was fully prepared to relinquish any and every association I had with him.

I know what you're thinking. *How could you feel that way about your own son, gay or not?*

I had a tough mindset, even being a teen-aged dad. I thought that I could at least solve the problem for the both of us. If he hated me he wouldn't want to see me, which was cool with me. I didn't want to see him walking around with a limp wrist anyway. I was at a crossroad without a compass, with no one to advise me on such an unorthodox situation.

Didn't most fathers disassociate themselves from their child, once they found out that they were going to like men?

I pushed back the wall, my son's gay future, with both hands, fighting, cursing, and questioning both God and my sanity. I'm old school and hard-headed with the way I think, believing I could change what was meant to be.

My experience should help any person that has someone in his or her life that lives differently, specifically if that person is your gay or lesbian child. Stereotypes attached to homosexuality have a staggering effect on society. I retained many of those stereotypes, I used derogatory terms, made queer jokes and laughed openly at any one living the alternative lifestyle. Ironically, the Universe thought it was appropriate to put me in the situation of having a gay son. Me... Eddie Wright... Street Entrepreneur... Ladies' man and hustler.

The critical point to be made here dear readers, was that as a black man, I, myself was being prejudiced against my own flesh and blood. As a Black man in America, that's a hard pill to swallow and very embarrassing to admit.

This book is meant to teach other fathers and all parents of gay children the lessons I learned the hard way, and should start a discussion on having a meaningful relationship between fathers and their children no matter whether they choose to live gay, straight, or somewhere in between.

This book is the "Voice for the Silent Fathers" for those going through the same thing I went through and my voice will be silent no more.

CHAPTER ONE

I was raised by my single, white mother in the suburbs of Suffolk County, Long Island along with my sister, Mimi who is 3 years older than me. Our African American father played a limited role in our lives. He moved back to Rochester, New York when I was two months old.

Visiting with my father for a few weeks in the summer wasn't enough to make a big impact on me. Let me correct that, it wasn't enough to instill the positive impact a young black male needs.

I wanted the type of dad that all of my friends had. The dad that took you to Yankees games, and stood in the yard throwing the football around, but my father never made much of an effort. It was like he wasn't interested in being involved with my life. Looking back to those early days, they were definitely a few contributing factors for me turning to the criminal lifestyle.

I promised myself that I would be the father I needed instead of the father I had. But who would have thought that fatherhood would propose such a catastrophe that I would start second guessing that very promise?

My son Drew was born September 20,1990. I don't know if homosexuality is a biological or mental condition. I never thought Drew would grow up making the conscious decision to be gay, the way other kids were making plans to become firefighters, police officers, or doctors.

When I would ask him what he wanted to be when he grew up, he would tell me all the normal kid choices, he never straight out said, "Dad, I want to be a gay ballerina dancer!" However, as a father with a keen street intuition, I sensed something abnormal was having an effect on Drew.

At a very young age, he began displaying mannerisms similar to his mother. He started sucking his teeth and rolling his eyes. He would tilt his head and alter his voice to imitate a girlish tone and it would get on my nerves. This was happening when he was around four or five years old, and I avoided paying too much attention to those signs for fear of re-reinforcing those flamboyant behaviors.

Around others, especially the women in Drew's life, I was depicted as "Mr. Macho." I was the bad guy who was always "over-reacting" when I addressed and attempted to correct certain mannerisms that just couldn't be ignored.

My "Gaydar" was active watching all his behaviors for a "Gayness Alert!" which would make me rush in, like the heterosexual swat team, to stop whatever he was doing and make it more boyish.

Other adults would tell me that my son would grow out of his feminine mannerisms, but what if he grew into them? No one had an answer for that!

I've heard a lot of theories in the media on what causes homosexuality, and although I'm not an expert and I don't have a degree in psychology or some other certification printed and framed, hanging dusty on display for all to see, I am the father of the gayest son on earth. When I say gay, I don't mean the quiet closet type, maybe that I could have handled. But no... The son that I was meant to father was doing Lady Gaga impressions in full drag queen attire while still in his mother's womb, born to show the world what being gay, proud and loud really meant, and lucky me, I had a front row seat.

Questions plagued my mind, searching for answers, maybe even a "cure" for my son's condition.

Was it in his genes? I don't remember having any gay relatives on my side of the family. Was it programmed into his D.N.A.? Or was my son choosing to be gay? If so, then I should've had the right to choose if I wanted a gay son, which of course I didn't. Show me a father who does. No one could really blame me for cutting off all ties if he chooses living life as a homosexual. Some people will even say that God justifies abandoning my gay son.

But really? Is that who I was going to choose to be? Isn't that what my father did to me? My mother had to take him to court to pay child support, while constantly nagging him to be more in me and Mimi's lives. Who knows? Who really even cared right then because I was trying to figure out what the fuck was I supposed to do with this baby that's captured my heart, whose mother is a spawn straight from hell that appeared to be doing all types of stupid shit in support of his sissy behavior. And what about my reputation to protect in these streets? How many gangsters got gay sons? None that I know of and I'd be dammed to be the first. I was torn with the emotional conflict with not knowing what to do. Especially at times when everything with my son would be normal as hell and out of nowhere Bam!! I was sucked right into the twilight zone.

CHAPTER TWO

The first time I saw Drew was three months after he was born, in front of the C-Town grocery store, with his mother Jennifer. She was pushing his stroller.

My girlfriend at the time, Rosa, was in the passenger seat of my black two door mustang, so I kept driving by with just that quick short glimpse of him.

Everyone I knew was asking if I was his father. Being immature, scared and naïve, I had my reasons why I denied it but my sister Mimi had been picking Drew up on the weekends since he was born, playing the aunt role, making the situation harder for me to ignore. After weeks of inner turmoil, and sleepless nights staying up wondering if I was Drew's father, I spoke with Mimi and agreed to get a closer look by spending some time with Drew.

As soon as I laid eyes on him, instinctively I knew. His tan skin, dark brown eyes, and beautiful smile made me understand why everyone said we were related, but at eighteen years old with my whole life ahead of me, I thought I was too young to be a father and deep down I knew I wasn't ready for that kind of responsibility.

My angel of a mother, who always stood by me through thick and thin, right or wrong, supported me but stayed neutral between myself and Jennifer. She always had a loving spirit for everyone. She's like a second mother to all of my friends growing up. So when she walked in the house to find me with a four-month-old smiling baby Drew, sitting together on the living room couch, she changed into Grandmother mode right on the spot, accepting Drew with open arms and a loving heart.

"Why hello gorgeous!" she said placing her purse on the chair then picking up Drew, carefully holding him close beaming her big grandmotherly smile which Drew reflected right back. They smiled at each other as he received a warm hug and a barrage of kisses.

Drew was an adorably cute baby; I'm not just saying that because he's mine either. He lit up any room and every person that came into contact with him couldn't help but smile. He was a beautiful child.

"Now this is one good looking boy" my mother said.

"Eddie" she joked "You were the best looking, but now you've been knocked down a notch by Drew here. By the way, thanks for making me a grandmother. I'm only in my forties you know."

"That's yet to be determined for sure ma" I had to let her know.

"Well thanks anyway son."

We shared some nice quality time with Drew, and Mom made the butterflies flipping around in my stomach disappear.

My mother was a social worker at Bay Shore Family Health Center, so she understood the difficulties that teen-aged parents faced. She made sure I knew that I wasn't alone. My mom always listened, neither agreeing nor disagreeing, when I would protest my doubts about being Drew's father... because it wasn't all peaches and cream. I'll explain...

First off Drew is named after one of Jennifer's ex-boyfriends, now put yourself in my shoes, how would you react? It bothered the hell out of me. I was upset, I had no say in the matter and I'm supposed to just be ok with that? I wasn't. So of course I questioned whether or not I was his dad despite his cute baby looks.

Naming a child after another man is a red flag.

Period.

Jennifer despised me because I denied being Drew's father, for reasons more obvious than that, so we had major parenting conflicts right from the beginning. I personally hated her for luring me into her life, making me believe I could trust her. She swooned in and took my virginity then betrayed me by sleeping with too many of my friends. Yeah, this chick was devious. Our relationship was poisoned and it affected how we parented Drew. She brainwashed him, with me as the bad guy.

There were too many times when I went to pick him up and he would scream, like really scream, at the top of his lungs "No, no, no! Please mama, please no! Don't make me, I don't want to go!" Tears would be flowing freely down his little red face.

My quick assessment made me feel like I was the biggest threat and since these guys weren't wearing masks, it wasn't a good position to be in. If they watched too many mafia movies they might shoot us all, leaving no witnesses. I wasn't in the mood to have my brains blown out over a Big Mac and Quarter Pounder.

They looked unsure of themselves and jittery, I had to speak and guide everyone through this. Eye to eye staring down the black tunnel of the shot gun barrel I asked...

"Yo! You guys want us to put our hands up?"

"Yeah" shot gun man replied "Everyone put your hands up!" he threw me a look, not sure what I was up to. We shared a moment of silence between us, I saw my shot to take control asking

"You want us to lie down on the floor?"

"Yeah " he said a bit more confidently raising his chin up a little.

So far so good, I thought, at least they haven't gone crazy yet. I could tell it was their first robbery, they were unorganized and out of sync with each other. The orchestration of this armed robbery in progress needed to go smoothly, so everybody could make it out alive.

Get.

Out.

Alive.

Period.

That became my plan, as I was sure my manager, who nervously did everything the other guy asked, didn't receive this kind of preparation training at McDonalds University.

The last thing I wanted was to die over some burgers and fries at the hands of two desperate amateurs, not much older than I was.

In a matter of minutes -of which seemed like several hours- they got the cash from the safe, draws, and night deposit, stepped over our bodies lying on the floor and left. I made myself a promise that night that I would never risk working in a legit job for someone else again.

That experience changed my perspective on life. I began taking the necessary steps, committing myself to being a hustler.

After graduating high school, making my mother extremely proud, I kept that momentum going by taking the liberal arts program at Suffolk Community College to give the appearance of being on the right track. All this academic work was a cover while accomplishing my goal... My main focus, building my criminal enterprise.

A few guys working for me took care of my business in the streets, keeping an eye on our block when I made time to be with Drew. I'll admit, once I pulled a cover move using Drew's innocence as a tactic in case I got pulled over with drugs in the vehicle and Murphy's law kicked in... Whatever can go wrong will go wrong, believe me. I did in fact get pulled over with him in the car coming back from meeting with my drug connect.

Facing twenty years in prison-that didn't concern me.

Thousands in drug money lost in the trunk, didn't faze me either.

Only one thing bothered me.

The thought of cops happily slapping the cuffs on me in front of a scared, crying, Drew broke my heart. So many thoughts ran through my mind, D.S.S workers would take Drew away from us, everyone would call me a piece of shit, my mother's heart would be broken.

But I was lucky that day. Promising myself never to take a risk like that again, I took my ticket and got my ass home.

I made sure no one in my family knew anything about the extent of my illegal activities, which ended up being a job in and of itself, but for me it was worth it. That was the last trip Drew ever took with me to do anything illegal.

CHAPTER THREE

"Eddie!" Drew's uncle Shawn yelled from upstairs. "Come up here now!"

Dashing off the couch, taking the stairs two at a time, I feared that Drew had split his head open, swallowed a plastic pen cap, or worse...

As if climbing Mt. Everest, Drew had just meticulously made his way up each of the eight wooden steps. Once at the top, he smirked back at me with a proud look of achievement, wearing only his diaper with a baby bottle of apple juice half full dangling from his little clenched teeth, then disappearing into the bedroom his Uncle Shawn was now yelling from.

Turning the corner, I ducked into the bedroom instinctively scooping up Drew inspecting him from head to toe, not seeing any visible blood, cuts, or signs of trauma. Glaring over at Shawn who was sitting on the far end of the bed, eyes fluttering between Drew and the floor.

I must've been missing something, what was I overlooking?

"What the hell happened?" I asked Shawn. He could only shake his head, at a loss for words.

"What are you yelling for Shawn? What's the matter?" It looked to me that there was more of a problem with Shawn than Drew.

"There's something wrong with your son," he answered not taking his eyes off the floor.

"Shawn," I demanded, "What's wrong with Drew?" Lifting him outstretched in front of me for a second more, thorough inspection for anything out of place other than his Uncle Shawn's odd behavior. I scanned his body from head to toe, checking for anything that I may have missed.

Shawn's eyes tried to look at me but shifted right back to the ground then to the window, looking off in some remote distance beyond the yards and houses, gazing into never-never land.

Exhaling, he finally blurted out, "I thought he was just settling in to watch TV with me when he crawled onto my lower back and..."

"What Shawn? Spit it out, what happened?" I was getting annoyed.

"Drew was stroking his diaper against my backside Ed!" He looked me dead in the face and continued, "and not in an innocent baby way either Eddie he..." He looked back down at his feet watching the front of his white Air Max sneakers, lifting a little, tapping them up and down nervously.

Drew had a plain look on his face as his eyes searched my own; puzzled, I looked back at Shawn and asked, "Hold up, what? Shawn!" I shook my head, "Did you just tell me that you were dry humped by my son?"

My mind raced thinking about what I thought I just heard. I would expect to hear that my dog Drama was dry humping, he shamelessly treated every stranger's outstretched leg like a two-dollar call girl, not my 18-month old son!

I needed answers, and I needed them fast!

I understood what he said clearly, but my brain didn't want to register what it was that he was telling me. In fact, I straight out rejected it. All I could do was display my confused eyes on Shawn, who, not answering, stood up and backed out the doorway as if I was holding the Anti-Christ in the fold of my arms.

Drew's homophobic Uncle Shawn was visibly shaken up and slightly shell-shocked from his encounter with Drew. Meanwhile, I stood there, stuck, perplexed at the whole situation.

My son was too young to be conscious of what he was doing, Shawn had to be exaggerating. I held my son closer to me, he smiled and laid his head against my chest causing me to relax a little knowing that he was physically okay. I rubbed his back and gave him a gentle parental kiss of reassurance, making the both of us relax.

An unsettling, bad feeling deep in my psyche made me think of what just happened, like an omen forewarning me of the future. My worst fears were on the horizon of my reality, as I couldn't totally shake what Shawn described. I was terrified but I chose to push it to the back of my mind.

Being a father, I learned, was more emotional, mental, and internal than just paying for stuff and changing diapers. Those last two things I could handle, but when Drew was almost three, his mother moved back to the Bronx to live with her father, a known sex offender. My nightmare scenario came true.

Jennifer, Drew's mother, was raised by her father until the age of fifteen, then she moved to Long Island to live with her mother. She told me that her piece of shit father did the unspeakable. He had been sexually abusing her since she was twelve years old. The fact that she was going back to live with this scumbag had me bugging out since now she had three-year-old Drew to look after.

Why would she go back?

God forbid anything happened to my son. Although Jennifer told me that everything was different now and all was safe and fine and blah-blah-blah, it still caused me many sleepless nights... Why should I trust that?

My mother's house on the other hand provided a stable environment with Drew's own bedroom, clothes, favorite toys and electronic games.

We did things that I wanted to do with my father. I would take Drew to get his hair cut, sitting him up in the booster seat. When the latest kid movies came out we were the first people sitting inside of the theater with a box of jumbo buttered popcorn, you know the wide circular box. He always insisted on holding it even though it took up his whole lap. We had every movie theater snack available, white snow cap candies, gummy bears, and an extra-large soda which Drew happily shared with me. Some of those outings at his age were the best days of my life.

I would load my pockets up with cash and spend most of it while out on our trips to Toys-R-Us. The type of stuff I dreamed about as a kid. I enjoyed every minute with Drew, living vicariously through his experiences, maybe even more than he did. Drew ran free, arms outstretched, with wild excitement down white linoleum polished floors, stepping on the lower level shelf reaching up for his favorite action figures and games. Gladly, I would pull them from the shelf and drop them in my cart.

He was spoiled, he got whatever the hell he wanted, and I loved every minute of it.

My happiness was his happiness and his also mine. He enjoyed my company, and I enjoyed his.

Emotionally I was now attached, even with a lingering possibility of me not being his biological father. As far as I was concerned, I was his protector, provider, and happily paid for all the things that came along with a growing toddler. I loved Drew.

My love for him was growing unconditionally stronger by the second.

One day when I took him to a brand new playground to have some fun, Drew came running back to our picnic table, on the verge of exploding into tears.

He talked.

I listened.

"Those kids won't let me play with them!"

Drew was visibly upset, tears welling up in his eyes.

He was hurt, which made me hurt, and unhappy, which made me unhappy. "Oh Yeah? Why not?" I asked raising up to fix this ordeal for my little prince.

Who do those kids think they are upsetting my son? I thought.

"Dad, they were just being very mean to me."

"Did you say they were being mean to you?" I asked.

"Yeah!" he said a little tough.

"Do you want me to go get those mean kids?" I asked

"Yeah!" he shouted a lot tougher, his almond eyes lighting up e electrified by our connecting confidence.

"Yeah dad," he was confident and ready for what was about to happen, he did a complete 180. The tears he just shed were now dry.

I curled my hands into fist, pounding one into the other open hand, and he copied me doing the same as we started our tough walk across the playground to confront these bullies who unknowingly were about to get a taste of their own medicine. Nobody messes with my son and gets away with it, nobody! I wanted Drew to know that firsthand from me, then and there.

Stomping towards the playground with a determined look on our faces, Drew pointed at the tormentors yelling, "There they are Dad. Get them!"

The kids momentarily stopped climbing the jungle gym hearing Drew's voice and looked at us, then back at each other, then back at us. They all looked to be under twelve but a lot older than Drew.

They all scrambled off the equipment to the ground, taking cautious steps backwards, their eyes widening, and mouths gaping open slack-jawed staring at the father and son with psychopath expressions jogging straight to them, sort of like when the male lion teaches his lion cub how to catch its prey for the first time.

My expression clearly said, "You wanna mess with my son?"

Big mistake, kids.

Big mistake. Run Kids! Run!

Turning on their heels they hauled ass into a full blown sprint cutting in different directions across green grass towards different corners of the park.

"You better run!" Drew yelled catching up with me as I slowed my pace. His little threat put a smile on my face. I didn't have a plan on what I would have done if those kids didn't run off, but Drew wanting me to beat up the bullies at the playground was normal boy behavior, which I was feeling good about.

Drew and I slowed down, taking our last few steps just walking triumphantly as the playground bullies scattered out of site. I looked down at my tough little man proudly.

This Drew who squinted his eyes tough, arms crossed, stood straight up almost cocky, watching the last kid turn into a small red shirt dot, running far down the side walk into the neighborhood.

I took a mental snap shot of this moment. Drew asking me to help chase off bullies.

Maybe there was hope of him growing out of his peculiar ways.

I tried to keep things as normal as possible. Growing up while other kids were going to Disney World, or the Caribbean Islands with their families for vacations, the best my mother could afford, being a single parent and taking care of two kids while putting herself through college, was taking us to the great outdoors, at different campsites on Long Island. I didn't hesitate introducing Drew to sleeping in a tent, building a fire, hiking in the woods, catching lightning bugs, waking up to smell the overnight ashes still warm from the burning down logs from the night before, then placing twigs on top blowing as hard as we could to bring the fire back to life without using a match.

Rosa, my girlfriend, and I would occasionally take Drew camping for the weekend, along with Rosa's younger sister Jackie. There were a number of different campsites to visit but we were regulars at Blydenburgh County Park, since it was only five minutes away from my mother's house.

If ever it seemed like Drew was bored, and I didn't have anything particular planned, instead of him sitting in front of the TV which he loved to do, I'd ask, "Do you want to go camping?"

Eyes wide and bright with a smile revealing his answer, he would lead the way downstairs into the basement where Grams kept a full stock of camping gear at the ready. Loading up the equipment in the trunk of the car, we'd then make a quick stop at the grocery store and an hour later the tent was pitched and the fire was roaring.

On one of these camping weekends with three-year-old Drew and Rosa, her sister Jackie, who was babysitting Jose, an 18-month-old baby boy, spent the day with us at the campsite. They had plans of dropping off Jose at home later that evening but figured spending the day out doors would keep both boys busy.

After playing on the swings, monkey bars and slides, collecting loose branches, sticks and various sizes of wood, Drew and I set out to keep the evening fire blazing.

"Dad the fire's too high for the food!" Drew pointed out.

"It will burn down in a minute"

"Did you remember to buy the marshmallows?"

"Of course, but you have to eat dinner first."

"Oh I will!" he answered.

After cooking hot dogs and hamburgers, the boys quickly ate and Drew helped Jose push the marshmallows down on the long sticks they collected for the moment.

"Watch out, it will go on fire and burn, Jose." Drew said standing next to Jackie who was holding Jose in her lap while roasting the marshmallows.

"That's the way I like to cook them," I said

"Burnt to a crisp, right Dad?"

"You know it!" I said sipping an ice cold Coors Light after swallowing a charcoaled-cooked marshmallow.

After finishing with the marshmallow roast, Jackie put Jose in the tent for a nap before taking him home. Drew followed close behind.

Twenty minutes passed before Rosa asked.

"Eddie, can you go get Jose?"

"Sure," I said as I got up from the lawn chair, finishing off the last gulp of another Coors Light.

Walking over to the tent, flipping open the flap, sticking my head in, I catch Drew giving another bumping and grinding performance, rubbing against Jose's diaper.

"What the hell!!" I yelled snatching Drew by his arm, pulling him off Jose and out of the tent.

"What's the matter?" Jackie asked running up behind me.

"Drew don't do that!" I yelled.

"What did he do?" Rosa asked as she looked in the tent, making sure Jose was ok.

"You don't do that!!" I repeated dragging Drew by his little arm over to my car, opening the back door and shoving him inside.

"Sit here!!" I barked, slamming the door as tears streamed down his face while he was yelling, "I didn't do anything!!"

Opening the door again, I yelled, "You know what you were doing was wrong. Stay here and think about it!"

Slamming the door again, I walked over to Rosa.

"Eddie, will you tell us what happened?" she asked while cuddling Jose in her arms.

"I don't know what's wrong with that kid, but he was doing his dry humping routine on Jose."

"Oh God!" Jackie said.

"Yeah!" was all I could muster, rolling my eyes looking down at the dirt floor.

"He's just mimicking what he's seeing, living with Jennifer," Rosa said.

"I don't know where he gets it from. Just take Jose home while I handle this."

"It's too dark to leave him in the car alone," Jackie said

"I'll be right here; I need to calm down. Go ahead and take Jose home."

After pulling away, standing alone by the fire, staring at the car, hearing the muffled sounds of Drew weeping, scared of the dark, sitting in the car alone, I wondered, *what am I supposed to do?*

Five minutes passed, I walked over with a mean look on my face, opened the car door for him to step out and see my angry expression, pointing at the tent I said, "Go straight to bed!"

"Daddy..."

"I don't want to hear anything! Just go to sleep!"

I walked him to the tent, opened up the flap, and Drew wandered in taking off his sneakers, climbing into his sleeping bag, curling up and closing his eyes.

Rosa returned to find me feeding the fire, finishing off the last of the 12-pack.

"Are you all right? Where's Drew?"

"That little monster is in there sleeping, " I said nodding my head towards the tent.

"Don't call him that; he's just a baby."

"No!" I barked. "Jose is a baby, Drew is three and shouldn't be molesting little boys!"

"Stop exaggerating Eddie."

"I'm telling you Rosa. There's something weird with him."

"No, there's not; he's just a child."

"Hmmm! Just a child." I retorted.

Hardly sleeping from feeling guilty because the way I handled the situation, as soon as I saw Drew crack his eyes in the morning, I unzipped my sleeping bag holding it open.

"Climb in," I said

Quickly crawling out of his sleeping bag, he snuggled himself in between my arms as I re-zipped the sleeping bag shut while giving Drew a big hug.

"Daddy, I can't breathe," he said with sour morning breath.

Releasing my embrace, for a few seconds I was silent, not knowing what to say.

"You know; I was very upset with you last night."

He nodded his head without saying anything.

"Don't do that again."

"Okay Daddy"

"You know I love you right?"

"Yeah Dad," he said with a smile. "And I love you."

CHAPTER FOUR

My mother encouraged me to be there for Drew on all levels, picking him up, spending time with him and forming new routines which started a new late night father and son snacking ritual. Hot Bagels, a 24-hour eatery became the source for our late night routine.

Before going home, I stopped to pick us up two cinnamon raisin bagels with cream cheese, grape jelly and two Snapple iced teas. The aroma alone would ease him gently, from his sleep. "Drew." I'd whisper. "Do you want to eat a bagel?" He would nod his little head yes before his dreamy eyes were fully opened. This was my favorite part about coming home, Drew and our bagels. We'd both dig in while happily watching each other munch away.

After a few bites and mini sips of our iced tea, he would ask, "Dad, can I come in your room and watch some TV?" As if on cue I'd respond, "Only if you keep the volume down so we don't wake Gram." Picking him up in one hand with his snacks in the other, we would both settle in on my bed, looking at the big screen. Drew always enjoyed watching late night cartoons on Nickelodeon.

This was my time to relax, shut down my body and sleep off the night before. By the time seven or eight rolled around, the time he would normally wake up re-energized, Drew would be winding down for a nap. It was perfect, I was able to catch up on the sleep I missed out on while running the streets, doing whatever I was doing.

*

When the weather was nice, in the summer, we had a spot on the roof where Drew and I would spend time talking and hanging out which was another ritual we enjoyed doing together.

I can remember one time, Drew was enjoying the heat from the sun he had his hands behind his head using his tee-shirt like a towel, sunbathing with his eyes closed as if he was at the beach, listening to me talking about trust.

"Drew, I want you to know that you might do things in life that get you in trouble or that you're not sure how to handle, and when you're in these situations, you need someone to trust that will help you. I'm your number one person, you can always trust me. You know that, right?"

"Yeah, Dad, - I know I can trust you because you love me so much, right?"

"Yes, that is right, I will never let anything bad happen to you or allow anyone to hurt you," I said.

"I know Dad, I trust you." He gave me a look that told me he wanted to but I wasn't fully convinced that he did.

When it came time to come down off the roof, we carefully made our way to the lower section of the roof where the yellow fiberglass ladder was, but I told Drew to wait as I pushed the ladder down to the ground.

Eyes wide with a smirk, Drew asked, "Dad, now how are we going to get down?"

"Like this," I said vaulting off the roof startling Drew, who stepped back in amazement.

"Whoa, Dad!" he exclaimed. "What do you think you are a Ninja?"

Ignoring the joke, I looked him dead in his eye telling him, "Jump to me Drew! I promise to catch you."

"What Dad?" he threw me a nervous glare. "I'm not crazy like you, it's too high!" He was naturally scared. "Drew, don't you trust me?"

"Yeah," he replied as he inched his way to the edge of the roof.

This section of the roof was only 10 foot or less which isn't that high for me being 5'7", but for a four-year-old kid, standing on top of it peering over its edge, working up the nerve to make the biggest jump in his life thus far, it probably seemed like a 50-foot drop.

He took several deep breaths leaning forward looking at my extended open arms, then back to the ground below.

"I will never let anything bad happen to you!"

Drew jumped off the roof like a little super hero, surprising me. As he crashed into my protective arms. With a bear hug and a smile, I congratulated him.

"You did it!!" We flashed our smiles at each other.

"Dad, I know I can trust you," he said. I lifted him up high in the air, spinning him around, triumphantly listening to the sounds of his laughter causing my own.

That was definitely a bonding day for the both of us.

I was proud of him, and he was proud of himself, but most importantly I now confirmed that he trusted me enough to overcome his fears.

We crossed a bridge of trust that some fathers and sons never get to experience, and that trust and confidence is so cemented in my heart that I still carry around until this day as if it happened yesterday.

*

As Drew grew, he became my mother's garage sale partner. The both of them went about it like modern day treasure hunts. When the fun was over, and it came time to bring Drew home to his mother's in the Bronx, he always wanted to come back, and we always looked forward to him being with us.

When he was three years old, I began another little ritual of letting Drew sit on my lap and play drive the car, heading up and down our dead-end street. During one of these rides I asked, " Do you like when your dad lets you drive the car?"

"Yeah, but you're not my real dad."

"What?" I asked blind-sided. "Who told you that?"

"My mother," he said flatly, lifting his chin matter-of-factly.

"Your mother, huh," I replied biting my tongue as my thoughts began racing, putting the pieces together of the Drew paternity issue that needed to be settled once and for all because if it didn't get resolved, I didn't know how much longer I could play house to a kid that might not be mine and by this point it wasn't just me that was attached to him, but my mom and Mimi also loved him as much as I did.

A little voice in the back of my head whispered, well yelled, *If Drew's not yours you're free! You can do whatever you want!* I turned the volume down on that thought and didn't say anything to anyone, not yet, since there was only one person I could tell about this.

As soon as I was back on Long Island, I burst through the front door, yelling to my mother what Drew revealed.

"Get the blood test, you've been avoiding," she said. "It will set your mind at ease."

I folded my arms and looked at her, we held each other's gazes a few moments, and she almost whispered to me, walking over placing her hand on my shoulder and repeated,

"It will set your mind at ease..."

She was right.

"Thanks Mom," I said and pulled her in for a big hug. I exhaled and instantly felt better.

"Ok, now let me make you something to eat," she said. "Are you hungry?"

"Actually, I am," I said, and I was. Making the decision to get the test was both scary and comforting. I was worried and excited.

If he wasn't mine, then my role as a dad, which I was growing into more and more comfortably on a daily basis, would vanish. But if he was, then I could settle in for the long haul and put this undecided nonsense out of my head once and for all.

Things looked up for me, and I was doing everything the right way, and on track, but my plans to get the test were interrupted by detectives knocking at my mother's front door one day with an arrest warrant that had my name on it. They were coming around for an alleged drug sale they thought I had something to do with.

Now as much as I wanted to clear this up and take care of my paternity business with Drew, facing the judge wasn't in my plans as I was already on probation for an alleged stolen car possession and some minor larcenies my friends and I did as youth offenders.

The next two years sucked, I was on the run playing hide and seek with law enforcement. Sneaking around. I still saw Drew on my days of visitation, if Jennifer allowed it. I didn't like being under her thumb like that, but what choice did I have?

Jennifer eventually moved back to Long Island with her mother but not before her tornado of destruction left a deadly impact in the Bronx.

Jennifer was 20 years old, pregnant and living with Drew and Michael, her 16-year-old boyfriend she ensnared. The damage she inflicted on my inexperienced heart in the past warned me that this innocent kid didn't stand a chance.

Here's how it went down.

Stephen, Jennifer's second son, was a six-month premature infant weighing less than four pounds and very fragile. Released after three weeks of care in the hospital and, after only two weeks' home, the worst nightmare a parent could have, came true. Stephen was found in his crib, dead. The autopsy confirmed he had died of Sudden Infant Death Syndrome also known as "SIDS."

The investigation into the whole situation invoking Stephen's death somehow revealed that Michael wasn't the father, but his best friend, who Jennifer was apparently sleeping with on the side, was.

Things unfortunately got worse as everything snowballed into a horrible end. Depression, betrayal, overwhelming sadness and anger for such a young, teen-aged, would-be father of a little boy was too much to bear on young Michael.

Soon after receiving the news that he wasn't the father, he confronted Jennifer in their bedroom, where unfortunately my son was sitting on the dresser a few feet away. Drew, just four years old, watched as Michael pulled a loaded handgun, placed it to his head, and in front of them both, pulled the trigger killing himself.

Worrying about Drew became my full-time job.

CHAPTER FIVE

Jennifer knew the shitty predicament I was in and used it to her advantage. The summons for Family Court couldn't be answered due to my outstanding criminal warrants, so she started manipulating my visitation time with Drew, which was eating me alive, but I found a way around it.

Nick and Rosie lived two blocks away from my mother's house. Jennifer befriended their daughter for a short time back in the day before Drew was born, and they treated him like he was their son. On weekends when Drew wasn't at my house, he was at their house, including when he was living in the Bronx.

They watched me grow up and knew me since I was in the fourth grade. Their oldest son Nick was one of my childhood friends; we rode B.M.X. bikes after school, played on the same soccer teams, and had sleep over parties. They always called me when Drew was there so I could pick him up and avoid dealing with Jennifer's bullshit.

They were outstanding people, sincere, stable and loved Drew so much that they spoke to me about adopting him if it turned out that I wasn't his dad.

Wow!

Talk about going above and beyond for a kid. They were every kid's dream parents, solid, grounded and supporting.

They used to give me short talks about the importance of stability for a child and the responsibility of being a parent.

Big Nick always looked out for me and never pushed too far which made his message easy to receive. He knew about my legal dilemma, being a court officer, and encouraged me to resolve my issues. He was one of the best role models in my life without realizing it, and I was lucky to have him in my corner.

Taking his advice, I had my lawyer arrange a date to turn myself in. I bumped into Jennifer a week prior to my surrender date. Flashing my headlights, I signaled her to pull her car over by mine on the same side of the street. Drew's grinning face from the back seat gave me a smile as I approached her driver's window. The scorn in Jennifer's eyes and sour face made my smile quickly disappear.

"Jennifer, let me take you to dinner tonight so we can clear things up. I don't want to continue to have problems with you." Drew reached out his arms for me to pick him up, which I did, cuddling my little man, my favorite person in the whole world, my real reason for turning myself in to settle this question of paternity once and for all.

"Hi, Dad!" Drew greeted. "I miss you."

"I miss you too, son." Looking at this kid who was happy to be in my arms made all the bullshit Jennifer threw at me worth it. But what if I wasn't his father? If the test results came back negative, what would happen to Drew?

"Hello... are you even listening to me asshole or what?" Jennifer's voice snapped my focus back to her unhappy face.

"I'll go to dinner with you, just put my son back in the car!" she demanded.

"Why don't you meet me at the park and ride at 5:45." I told her. "I don't want a show down with the wicked witch of the west... I mean you mother." My attempt at humor didn't penetrate her thick skull as the look in her eyes told me that I was walking on thin ice.

"I'll drop Drew off and meet you there," she confirmed. "I got something to get clear with you also." We locked eyes just for a second, and I didn't like what I saw behind them. What was she up to? What was she hiding?

*

Being on the run for two years kept me alert and cautious, some might have called me paranoid.

I arrived at the park and ride twenty minutes early, scoping the scene out, keeping my guard up ready for anything.

Three cars passed by, all the drivers slowing down just enough to get a good look at me before speeding off.

Jennifer pulled up almost on cue seconds later.

"Jump in my car. I'll drive to the restaurant," I told her.

Shooting a nervous glare up the street she said, "I have to wait for my mother to bring me Drew."

"I told you I didn't want to deal with your..." a bad feeling overwhelmed me. "I'll be back," I said throwing the car in gear and pulled off to leave.

"What the fuck was I thinking trying to clear things up with a crazy chick like..."

The three cars I saw earlier pulled next to Jennifer, cutting off my train of thought, followed by a regular blue and white patrol car, which Jennifer waved in my direction.

I knew it! I punched the steering wheel disgusted. *Fucking bitch!!*

The cop pulled alongside of me with the lights flashing, screaming out to me through his open passenger window.

Spending two years ducking the law, being less than a week away from surrendering, the last person I would allow to get credit for turning me in would be Jennifer.

I'd rather hit a brick wall head on doing 100 mph than let Jennifer have the satisfaction of having me busted, and after all I've done for that ungrateful...

Saying that I was upset was an understatement. Locking the doors and turning up the tunes, which happened to be Nas' Illmatic album, I flashed a smirk at the cop and hit the gas.

The brand new Accord shot across the double lanes onto traffic. The rearview mirror showed the cop was on my tail, along with a grab bag of law enforcement as back up.

The engine roared as the rubber grabbed concrete screeching around a series of sharp turns throughout residential neighborhoods, keeping my speed jacked up as long as I didn't hit a traffic jam as only one thought crossed my mind.

I'm not stopping until I get away!

And I didn't, losing them after some risky driving, endangering my life and scaring the crap out of a few people that I nearly hit. I needed a pay phone.

Every criminal in America knows there's only one person you can trust when you're on the run. She picked up after the second ring.

"Are you ok, son?" she asked.

"You won't believe what happened. I tried to make peace and talk with Jennifer before going to jail, and she tried to set me up! Can you believe that bitch? But I got away!" I explained.

"I already know, Eddie. The police came here saying Jennifer told them you tried to take Drew from her earlier this afternoon. Go to your uncle's house and stay there. The police are driving up and down our street," she warned.

I laid low at my uncle's for the next few days and turned myself in as planned. I looked forward to Court for the paternity test.

But first I had to confront the Judge in my criminal case.

*

Sentencing day!

Time to receive my fate.

Mr. Nick stood behind the Judge giving me a wink and a head nod.

I appreciated it. It was cool but everyone knows when you're standing in front of the Judge about to be sentenced-it's nerve wracking. Some won't admit it-some will try to look cool and confident while it's handed down-but most will tell you it's a gamble.

I looked at the Judge.

"Mr. Wright I now sentence you to..." He looked at me.

I glanced over my shoulder, and in that flash before looking back at the Judge, seeing my mother standing proud in the audience with her vigilant stare, leaving no room for doubt that it was her beloved son before the Court.

"Eight months at the Riverhead County Jail and will grant you 4 months' jail credit in exchange for the 450 hours' community service completed while on probation."

"Thank God!" Someone said behind me.

The lawyer stepped beside me and began his spiel about getting me the time off, but I'm sure Nick's whisper to the Judge's ear had something to do with my merciful sentence.

Four months flew by, and once released, my lawyer set the date for the blood test with Family Court.

When the day came and my blood screen test finished, Jennifer made a petition to the Court requesting supervised visits with Drew.

Are you fucking kidding me? I thought. I'm here taking the test, and I don't see any other would-be dads in line to raise a child with a combative bitch of a mother like this at the ready to open his wallet and pay his way!

My anger fueled me to speak up.

"Excuse me Your Honor, Drew's been well taken care of by me and my family on the weekends for the last 4 years. I'm not denying he's my son, just making sure. That's why I'm taking this test, but supervised visits?" I explained, "Your Honor, there's no need, I don't think she..."

"But he's a drug dealer!" Jennifer cut in, interrupting, ratting out my illegal career to the Judge, and on top of it, telling her I was fresh out of prison.

Jennifer displaying her true colors in front of everyone.

I didn't react or say anything, but I did think about all the times I put cash in her hands and it was all smiles and ice cream... The Judge just looked at both of us thoughtfully. My grief must have been all over my face. How many fathers a month, week, day stood in front of her bench and fought off the wrath of baby mama drama like this? She took pity on me and denied Jennifer's request for supervised visits. "Bitch!" I think she mumbled under her breath although it wasn't clear.

Jennifer wouldn't let Drew out of her grasp; I couldn't help sneak smiles at Drew when she wasn't looking. She was being a relentless you know what, and out in the parking lot I took a few quick steps to catch up with her and tried attempting peace again.

She gave me the *Are you for real?* Ice Queen eyes but stopped long enough to hear me out.

"I really miss Drew." I said directly to him.

"Can I come with you, Daddy?" he asked with all the cuteness of a child his age.

"It's fine with me," I said looking at Jennifer with every good intention. "But, it's up to your mother."

Drew's irresistible smile was aimed at Jennifer, also waiting for a response.

There we were, father and son pleading with this woman who hates me, for us to be together.

I could hear the silent few seconds while she decided, banging in my chest like a drum.

The next thing I knew; Drew's being passed into my arms for the weekend. I was all smiles strapping him into the backseat. We were going to have lots of fun.

*

As soon as I saw the envelope I knew what it was...

Paternity test results. I jogged up the steps, into the house to answer the ringing phone.

"Hello?" I answered ripping out the letter confirming Drew's mine.

"Did you read your mail yet?' Jennifer asked

"Yeah, lucky for you it turned out the way it did."

"Whatever Eddie,'" she said. "I just wanted to make sure you know."

"I do," I said. "But, thanks for your concern."

Click!

My rising body temperature turned my face flush red, anxiety building up in my chest was bursting to explode out.

I sat down in my mother's love seat.

Took a breath in.

Closed my eyes, rigid, I tried to relax.

Exhale.

Only one message was clear to me at that moment.

I'm going to have to deal with this demented bitch for the rest of my life.

For a brief moment, getting hit by a bus didn't seem like such a bad idea.

I unclenched my teeth, rubbed my fingers through my low fade, grasping for hair to pull and read the letter for the third and final time.

Leaving Drew's life wasn't an option, but I knew deep inside that I was already too emotionally invested to abandon that boy no matter what that test result letter confirmed.

One side of my mental balance saw Jennifer wearing me down with her bullshit until I lost my sanity. The other side of that balance looked forward to being in Drew's life although dealing with his rising girlish alter ego was troublesome.

This is good news.

I'm Drew's father! I thought

"I'm Drew's father," I said trying it out loud.

Drew's... Father...

"Eddie call me"

I snapped out of my over thinking and called the person who whispered in my mind, my best friend and corner stone in my life.

She picked up on the first ring.

"Hello Mom?" I got the results of the paternity test.

My mother's slight gasp sounded like a surprised breath.

"Drew's my son, I'm his father and you're his grandmother." I told her in my most upbeat voice I could muster.

"Thank God Ed that's great news!"

"You know mom," I said. "I love Drew with all my heart I do- but dealing with that bit..."

"Well, son," she cut in at just the right time keeping me from getting too upset. "We've dealt with her for this long, were going to be fine, plus Drew is worth it."

"He is worth it mom," I said.

"Be proud that he's your son, Eddie"

"I am Mom, I am."

Drew fit right in as he's a funny kid that always attracts attention to himself especially with his mannerisms which were embarrassing for me, but so far so good today. Just normal kid fun and I was cool with that.

The party was wrapping up and party bags were being passed out to all the kids, blue for the boys and pink for the girls. Drew politely asked for a pink party bag, I stepped in between Drew and Vinny's Mother, crouching down smiling saying, "Drew the pink is for the girls, take the blue one..."

"Pink is my favorite color!! I want a pink one!!" he whined, staring at me defiantly.

"Drew, I don't think you should..."

"Pink! Pink! Pink! I want the pink one dad. It's my favorite color!"

The attention in the bowling alley shifted to the two of us and it seemed as if even the music that was playing stopped.

My face was turning red and I was feeling the rise of embarrassment heat up my body temperature. Vinny's mother's eyes met my own. She saw my situation and knew I was stuck.

Shaking my head, I asked defeated, "Could he please have a pink one?"

She saw me barely holding it together as my eyes gave away the pain I didn't express or need.

"Sure you can have a pink one, Drew," she said with a reassuring smile passing him the party bag and giving me a pat on the back, as I got ready to leave.

"I have a pink one, I have a pink one, I have a..."

All the way out the front door and to the car he chanted over and over like some kind of childlike mantra.

I walked as fast as I could to the car never looking back, hurrying Drew inside, and buckling him in the back seat. I made my way to the driver's side, unclenching my teeth, getting in, I spun around, speaking sternly I said, "Drew!" with all the intentions of scolding him, but when he looked up so innocently shaken from my tone, holding his pink party bag, that he was so happy with, it just melted all my anger away.

I took a deep breath and said smiling,

"Did you enjoy yourself?"

"Yeah, Dad. I had a great time."

I drove us home and never brought it up again.

CHAPTER SEVEN

Five-dollar bags purchased in New York City sold for twenty dollars in Ocean View, Virginia.

Cold.

Hard.

Cash.

Fast.

I was making money hand over fist, and I couldn't keep enough product. Virginia here I come!

For those two years on the run, Ocean View, down in the Norfolk area, became my home base of operations. There were a lot of perks.

Rent was cheap for one. Beautiful woman were always laid out on the beaches, walking through town, smiling and extra friendly. If there ever was a place to hide out from the cops, this was it.

Peppy was my close friend going back to my Junior year in high school. We got in all kinds of trouble as young boys. We became youth offenders for different crimes, including a couple of alleged robberies, which just being accused of, was enough to get us kicked out of St. John's High School. He was my running partner, and we went into full blown hustle mode, falling into a routine that we both knew well.

My hands tightened hard around the steering wheel. I bit my lip and kept silent a few minutes not wanting to take it out on Drew. Saying I was mad was an understatement. Furiously disappointed would be close. I'm not sure how to label my thoughts but it was enough to call Jennifer and speak my mind as soon as Drew was playing outside safely out of ear shot.

She picked up on the third ring.

"Can you please tell me what the hell is going on?"

"Going on with what, Eddie?"

"With you eating pussy, Jennifer!" I accused continuing "What, are you trying to purposely make Drew gay?!"

"Fuck you!!" she shouted, hanging up on me in usual Jennifer style.

Language fails to describe my anger.

I pressed the redial button and counted backwards from 10.

She picked up when I got to four.

"Jennifer I couldn't care less about your personal life but your girlfriend situation is going to affect Drew and I don't think..."

"You worry about Drew when he's with you, no one, especially you Eddie, can tell me how to raise my son!"

"Jennifer," I pleaded. "If you shape his brain this young with your lesbian bullshit, he's going to turn out to be..."

Click.

All I could do was shake my head, and not smash the phone against the wall like my brain was telling me to. The angry part of my mind, luckily I kept in check, which is almost impossible when dealing with Jennifer.

Placing my hands on the sink I looked out the window, took a deep breath, and relaxed some, watching Drew and Vinny climbing the big Oak with its long, reaching limbs, sitting where it forks off.

I used to play on that same tree. I thought.

How simple life is for those kids I mused almost wishing to go back in time and be a kid again myself as I watched the boy's spider monkey up and down the ancient oak, without a care in the world.

*

"Mom, this girl is destroying Drew and there's nothing I can do to save him."

"You just have to continue to be a loving father and everything will work out."

"A loving father?" I wanted to pull my hair out.

"If Drew ends up being gay, I'm not going to be his father at all! I won't want nothing to do with him bringing boyfriends to the prom or worse...marrying one!"

"Ed!" she pleaded. "You're overreacting, it's too soon to tell whether he'll be gay or not, regardless of how he turns out, he's your son and you still have to love him."

"Mom," I questioned stepping closer to her to make my point. "Are you crazy? Do you hear yourself?"

"Ed, now listen you just need- "

"No! You listen Mom, please look at it from my point of view. I wasn't raised in the 60s with you and all your hippy friends preaching love, peace and happiness. I live in the real world, in a man's world, where if a boy wants to be gay, then he doesn't want a father!"

"Ed, come back here!" She yelled as I stormed up the stairs, ignoring her, into my room slamming the bedroom door behind me.

I laid on my bed, over the covers, sneakers on, hands behind my head taking deep breaths for about twenty minutes clearing my head of all the anger and frustration. Thoughts of upsetting my mother pulled me out of bed, pushed me out of the bedroom and down the stairs to find her poking at the cuticles of her nails causing them to bleed.

Damn, I felt like a jerk treating the only person who's always there from me through thick and thin the way I did.

I needed to fix things.

Swiping her hands to make her stop, I bent over to give her a hug speaking softly, "Sorry, Mom. I didn't mean to get you upset."

"I know son, you're angry, and it's a difficult situation, but you'll be fine."

I wasn't too sure about that but I kept my opinion to myself.

*

The whole gay son issue was the furthest thing from my mind back in Virginia; crossing the Chesapeake Bay Bridge was like returning to a normal reality after having been living in the twilight zone.

"They had their pajamas on," Robin said down playing the whole situation. "They're only kids, they were just playing," she said acting as if it was nothing.

"Just playing?" I almost shouted continuing "dry humping Josh who was just expecting to play video games and eat pizza instead getting grinded. You see why I told you to keep an eye on him? What's wrong with this kid?" I said almost ripping the door off the fridge reaching for a Heineken.

"Calm down," Robin said rubbing my back. "They were just playing and then he cried himself to sleep."

I spun away from her soothing hands not wanting affection until I made myself clear.

"Can you please tell me what they were playing? He cried because he knows what he's doing is wrong, and I've caught him doing that shit before!"

"Quiet down, he might hear you and I don't want to wake them," she said.

"I don't care if he hears me, as a matter of fact, I'm ready to wake him up right now and drive his perverted ass back to his mother's where they can both live their alternative lifestyle together in their own alternative world without me in it!"

"Eddie, you're upset and not thinking clear, have another drink and come relax with me on the couch," she said passing me a Grey Goose and cranberry juice on ice.

I gulped it down, twirling my hand in a small circle, signaling for a refill, sliding her the empty glass as the warmth sunk down the center of my chest. Drew's actions burst my bubble of normality that living in Virginia offered. I just wanted to get him back to his mother's. After a night's rest to think about it, the following morning I didn't want to send Drew off on a bad note so I didn't mention the incident, said our good byes, and I peeled off back to Long Island.

I kept my mouth shut but it was bothering me inside- like a bad feeling I couldn't shake off. It became a planted seed embedded in the back of my mind that never went away and only grew bigger like a tumor as time went on.

The more it ate me up from the inside, the more I tried to pour alcohol down my throat to kill it. This condition was stealing my Drew away from the life he was supposed to have, the life we were supposed to have, and my only plan was to drown out the pain of this condition from the inside was with an endless amount of booze.

And that's exactly what I did.

CHAPTER EIGHT

Drew's entire situation was frustrating. Now that he knew I was busy with the clothing store, I used it as an excuse for not spending time with him. On some level, I knew this was wrong but I was still sorting out my feelings about the state of affairs with him and I figured it was better to create some space between us rather than being the bad guy to him when I came around because I wasn't happy with his behavior.

When I drove up to New York it was to handle business and check in with Rosa. One night, I was picking her up from dinner, she slammed the car door when she got in, turned off the sounds of S.W.V., and even ignored me when I leaned in for a kiss. She fastened her seat belt and she stared straight ahead without saying a word.

"Okay" I shook it off and threw the car in drive. Pulling to the corner of her street, making a right turn heading to our favorite Chinese restaurant "Hau-Pu's."

Getting sick of the silence between us, I turned the music back on, only for her to shoot out her arm and snap the power button back off, giving me a seething stare that could melt ice, daring me to touch it again.

"Is it that time of the month already?" I asked watching her recoil back into the passenger seat ready to pounce at any moment.

I wasn't putting up with this silent shit, I thought, pulling up in front of the restaurant. Leaning against the driver's door, facing her I asked, "Should we even bother going inside?"

"Yes, you have me starving, " she growled, getting out on her own, slamming the door in my face.

Like I didn't have enough problems, I thought shaking my head. I looked up for a quick moment to question the God I couldn't see. I smirked to myself, got out of the car, and raced around to the main entrance just in time to pull the door open for Rosa as she walked in, hugging her chest.

Making $50 a day for a kid my age may as well have been $50,000 as it taught me that I didn't need to rely on my mother to buy things for me. I learned the basics of economics, the value of a dollar, and most importantly, the benefit of working hard and having a hustle, and I liked that.

More than ever I was determined to spend every day of the summer sitting on that hard green metal golf bench until every last soda was sold. What better way to spend a summer? I know, I know, I could have spent those days playing sports, riding my bike around with all the other neighborhood kids... but those kids didn't have 50 bucks a day in their pocket to buy whatever they wanted.

It seemed worth it to me.

For a bonus, at the end of the day, as the sun began to set with no more golfers in sight, I would take off my sneakers and socks and wade into the muddy-bottomed water traps. As the mud swished between my toes, I felt around with the fear of some unforeseen water monster like a snapper turtle or giant snake biting off my toes, in the search of every golf ball I could find without drowning. I cleaned them up at home and sold them right back to the golfers along with the sodas the next day.

My entrepreneur skills only got sharper as the summer transited into the new school year in September. I invested my money in Blow Pops, Red Hot Fireballs, and whatever else I could buy for a nickel, reselling them for a quarter each.

It was a skill I would carry with me for the rest of my life. The clothing store was another business venture that my mother encouraged.

Although...

She knew nothing about the illicit dealings that happened in the backrooms of Northern Exposure spelled back then with the letter "X" as in Xposure.

I thought it was cool, but it was just smoke and mirrors to wash all the incoming cash, and as you now know, if it made a quick profit, I considered it and probably did it.

The bad thing at that time was having my mother on the war path hunting down everyone and anyone who would somehow corrupt her beloved son.

No one was safe.

Not my business connects.

Not my girlfriends.

Not even me.

"Baby, I met your mother! She's so sweet!"

"I know Robin, but I called to remind you that she will rock you to sleep to find out what she wants to know. She's smart, Robin. Like C.I.A. interrogator smart and I don't think it's safe to- "

"Well, too late, Eddie. I'm sorry to be the one to tell you this but your mother's already on the hunt since she got here this morning!"

"What happened? Robin, what did she do? Where did she go? Tell me, Robin, what did she find out and where was she?"

"She found out where your father was staying and had a long talk with him."

"It wasn't a talk Robin; it was an interrogation! Why didn't he leave when he had the chance? I warned him!"

"Eddie, he didn't think she would find his apartment so fast but she did..."

"Of course, she did! She has the nose of a blood hound and the instincts of a bounty hunter! I told him to leave right away!" I was pissed.

"Well, he didn't, and that's not all Eddie, it gets worse..."

Sweat popped all over my nose and forehead, and I felt the temperature swell up all around me.

"Eddie, maybe today's not a good day to hear."

"Spit it out, Robin!!"

"When she finished with your father, she went over to the weed spot, and kept banging on the door until..."

"Tell me they weren't crazy enough to let her in..."

"Eddie, maybe..."

"Robin, you better not say those dumb asses opened the door."

"Eddie, it's your mother and she either scared them or maybe it was out of respect for you!"

"For me? No they were scared, what happened?"

"Once they opened the door, she stormed in, flipped over the table with all the weed, scales and cash on it, threw folding chairs at the workers, and screamed at the top of her lungs demanding to know who was running the operation. Once she found out, she slammed one of the guys against the wall, ripped out his earring, crushed it with her foot and told them to pack their shit and get out of town, or she was coming back and next time wouldn't be so nice. They're shook!"

Closing my eyes, I pictured the whole scene.

Like a movie...

Door kicked in...

It seemed like weeks before Saturday arrived. I began to call the store every twenty minutes from 8:00 am until 12:00 p.m. when he finally answered.

"Yo, Pep! What the fuck is going on?"

"Those punk mother fuckers tried to put their murder game on for real!"

"For what reason? Why?" I asked.

"Who knows, they started acting funny once you got locked up."

"But what problems were you guys having?"

"Nothing that called for this, I'm telling you Eddie...I think your Mom had something to do with it."

"My mother!! Are you crazy?"

"Nah, not like she told them to do it, but she told me that she would make me pay... Look what she did to your father! She probably cast a spell on us both!"

"Peppy, get a hold of yourself. Do you hear the shit you're saying? My dad died from a heart attack."

"Your Mom's a witch."

"Cut the shit," I said as I began to laugh at this entire situation.

"You think it's funny because you know I'm right. First your father and then this with me, what more proof do you need?"

"I think it's funny because you sound hysterical, now how you holding up? How's your hand?"

"My hand is fine, it was a scratch but they were gunning at me, I'll give them that."

"Well, what's next?"

"I'm packing up the store and moving to Maryland with my sister. I'll open up out there. Things just don't work out here without you."

"All right, do what you got to do to stay safe."

"What I'm going to do is find a voodoo lady to cast a protection spell from your Mom."

"Yo, Pep, you're really too much. I'll call you at your sister's in a few weeks."

Peppy was way too superstitious to try to convince him to keep things in operation. A part of me was relieved for no longer having to worry about those outside responsibilities. I had enough to focus on with these charges.

After eleven months spent in the Virginia Beach County Jail, I was sentenced to 4 years in State Prison.

CHAPTER ELEVEN

After leaving the Virginia Beach Jail and being sent to Deep Meadows Prison to be classified for three months, I was designated to Lawrenceville Prison, a brand new maximum-security facility.

I only had one question for my potential cellmates living with me in a 2-man cell, "Do you fuck with boys?"

If they answered "yes", then they weren't living in the same cell as me and would have to find another place to live. If there was a problem with having to move, then we would have to knuckle up as I refused to live with any type of homosexual.

Prison is an environment where homosexual activity is prevalent. There are openly gay men that look, dress, and act like women, but the majority of them either kept it on the down low or were unaware that their activities were characterized as homosexuality.

Damon, my cellmate from Baltimore, Maryland had a light skin black complexion like myself, was 22 years old with a 7-year prison term and was ready to fight just because I asked him that one question since he was also homophobic.

Damon's friend Mark, who was from Washington D.C., swore he was a ladies' man, always brushing grease in his hair to keep his waves tight and shiny. One afternoon Mark came in our cell bragging about getting a blow job by one of the openly gay men in our unit. Damon and I both looked at him like he was insane.

"You let a man suck your dick Mark!!" Damon said after a moment of stunned silence.

"Yeah, ain't nothing wrong with that, he knows what he's doing, too. He's only charging two packs, but you red bone mother fuckers, he'd probably do for free." Mark answered as if he was expecting us to run out of our cell to follow his suggestion.

Damon jumping off the top bunk, shouted, "Mark, we don't fuck with no fags!"

"Eddie, what's wrong with him? You down right?'

"No! I'm not down, and there ain't nothing wrong with Damon or me, we're not homosexuals." I said knowing my insinuation was loud and clear.

"I'm not a homosexual!" Mark protested.

"Oh, yes, you are!" Damon quickly replied.

Mark was flushed with an angry expression and quick to defend his statement.

"Just because I let him suck my joint don't make me a homo!" he refuted.

"Let's look up homosexual in the dictionary and see then." I said pulling out the Webster's from the desk cubbyhole.

It read: "Homosexual: Having any sexual desire to persons of the same sex."

"Getting your dick sucked by another man means you're a homosexual."

Damon factually stated, as he and I laughed at Mark who shook his head, biting his bottom lip, looking towards the floor while we were clowning him.

"Hell, no! That ain't what it means!!" Mark protested.

"Whether you're pitching the ball or swinging the bat, you're still playing the same game," I said grabbing my stomach to ease the pain from laughing so hard.

Damon and I slapped hands as Mark stormed out of the cell while Damon shouted, "Ain't nothing but real men up in here!!"

That wasn't the only time we proved our point with the Webster's dictionary.

The prison environment made me aware of how common homosexuality is. Walking the yard one sunny mid-summer day after doing pull-ups with a guy named "Outlaw"-who had completed a 10- year stretch then went to the streets for 11 months, and came back with a fresh 25-year sentence- was boasting all about the women he was with when he was home.

"Eddie, I was fucking 2 or 3 women a day, I was a pussy magnet, and they couldn't get enough of the Outlaw."

"After doing 10 years I'm sure you couldn't get enough of them either," I said walking around the curve on the asphalt track.

"Shit, I got enough of them. One night I was just so tired of pussy, I went up to the strip and got me a boy," he stated as a matter of fact.

"What!" Stopping mid-step confused. "I know you didn't just say you fucked a man Outlaw."

"Sure did, he had a fat ass, too."

"Oh, shit! I didn't know you got down like that."

"I sure do, ain't no shame, young blood."

"Not for you I guess," I replied.

"You ain't never had a boy?"

"No! And never will my man because I ain't gay."

"I ain't gay either, I still like women."

The conversation ended as we finished our lap, and me making a mental note to never work out with Outlaw again. Who knows what type of thoughts he had while spotting me during those last few sets of pull-ups. The surprising thing is that after the initial shock, I wasn't surprised.

I was civil with all the openly gay men, especially when it came to my prison hustle. I ran a store box, selling mostly cigarettes, which was used as the main currency in prison. I give one pack for two in return the following week. I was always careful about how much credit to give and who to give credit too, especially in this dangerous environment. The ones I never had to worry about were the openly gay men. Their money was always guaranteed with all the prostitution going on so they had unlimited credit with me.

Cece, an openly gay man, was one of my best customers. He was a gossip queen, always telling me who owed him or who he was going to get packs from to pay me back, knowing I knew how he earned his money. We had a cool enough relationship that I asked him questions one day as I grabbed the Newport's he ordered.

"How old were you when you knew you were gay, Cece?"

"For as long as I can remember," he replied in his feminine voice.

"Were you raised by a bunch of women?" I asked.

"Child, please, I have 5 older brothers, 2 younger brothers, and 1 younger sister."

"So your father was in your life?"

"Yeah, until I told him I was gay and he hasn't spoken to me since," Cece said sounding more hurt than angry.

"How old were you when you really knew?"

"I always knew."

"But how old until... You know?"

"What? When I had my cherry popped?"

"If that's what you call it."

"I was fifteen, why? You finally ready to take a ride on the wild side?" he said with a jokingly smirk.

"Get the fuck out of here, Cece! I'm asking because I think my son might be headed to that wild side."

I recognized the sincere concern in the way his expression changed once I mentioned Drew. Pointing at Drew's picture on my wall, he asked, "That's your son right there?"

"Yeah, that's him."

"He sure is a cutie, just like his dad."

I paid no attention to his flirtatious comment. "How can you expect your father to accept you being gay?'

"The same way my mother did."

"But a mother is different than a father, he's a man, and if Drew turns out to be gay, I can't see myself being in his life."

"Well, it would be your loss sugar! If you really love him, you'll accept him, and I can see that you do from reading the color of your aura."

"Cece, get the fuck out of here with your energy reading shit," I said.

"For real, Eddie, it's hard enough in the world for us. I would have given anything for my father's support."

"I'm sure your father would have given anything for you not to be gay." I shot back.

"Well I'm queer and here, accept it and respect it!" he said, taking his 2 packs of Newport's, spinning around and strutting away like some runway model.

I didn't have a problem with how another man chooses to live their life, my issue was with Drew.

Prison exposed me to aspects of the culture gay men shared. They had a common language, speaking Pig-Latin fluently, especially when they wanted to talk about you when you were nearby. I was able to pick up on it from remembering when my sister used to speak it with her girlfriends when we were younger.

They stuck together like any other click or gang, so if you messed with one, you would have to worry about all of them and their boyfriends.

Just because homosexuality is openly accepted it didn't create homosexual tendencies within straight men.

I've known plenty of convicts with life sentences that never thought about messing with another man, and I've known guys with a few months to serve, engage in homosexual activities.

If a person uses prison as an excuse, their homosexuality must have been hidden or repressed and once in an atmosphere so readily accepting, they no longer feel the need to hide.

Reading a book called "The Right Thing to do" by James Rachels, I came across an essay labeled 'Is Homosexuality Natural?' It claimed that the statics they had revealed that almost half of all American men have participated in homosexual activity during a period in their lives, and that a large percentage of these men had exclusively homosexual relationships for quite some time. Based on their statics homosexual behavior was natural, at least according to their sense of the word natural.

At one period in my life, I would have found that quote hard to believe but now since it was my own son who was in question, I began to look at things differently.

CHAPTER TWELVE

Around two years into my sentence, Robin abruptly stopped answering my letters, wouldn't accept my calls, and didn't come to visit.

I was never disillusioned with my expectations with the circumstances of our relationship, but it still hurt like a mother fucker! On my 26th birthday, I paid one of the CO's a pack of cigarettes to use the phone in the counselor's office to call Robin direct. I wasn't very optimistic.

"Hello?"

"Robin, what the hell is going on? Why haven't you answered my letters or anything?"

"Oh, my God! Where are you calling from?" she answered with her own questions avoiding my own.

"I escaped to find out what happened to you," I joked.

"I can't believe I'm hearing your voice, Eddie."

"Believe it! What the fuck happened? Did you get pregnant and have a baby?"

After a short pause and a slight sniffle from a tearful breath she answered...

"Yes."

"Well happy birthday to me!" I said slamming down the phone after feeling like I got kicked in the gut. Robin had been the only person I stayed in contact with besides my mom and talking with Drew on the weekends at her house.

At least once a month my mother took the 8-hour drive to visit, and although she had just been down the previous weekend, when I called her on my birthday with a shattered heart, she filled the gas tank and hit the road.

Visitation was completely different from the county jail. In a big open room, we're able to sit at our own table, buy food and spend from 8:30 am until 2:30 pm together. Mom would drive down the night before, get a little rest at a local hotel and be the first one in the door.

Entering the visiting room seeing her smiling face made all the recent worries from my broken heart vanish.

"Hi, Mom," I greeted, grabbing her in a warm embrace.

"Hi, Son, it's good to see you."

After our normal pleasantries and 2 hours of conversation, she gently eased her way into the topic of Jennifer.

"Jennifer's new baby daughter Alexis is just adorable," she said.

"I'm sure she is. Drew sounds like he enjoys being a big brother."

"Yes, Eddie, he does. Just watching him interact with her brings joy to my heart."

"I really miss Drew and look forward to seeing him, Ma."

"He misses you too; you'll be home soon, son."

"Yeah, we're half way there," I said giving her a wink and reassuring smile.

"You know; I've been meaning to tell you that Jennifer's been asking about coming with me to visit you."

"Why?"

"I don't know, Ed. You do share some history together and a child; she's working on getting her life together."

"What's that got to do with me?"

"Who knows maybe nothing, but since Robin's no longer coming to visit, I figured it might be a good time to work on being more friendly with one another. It would be better for Drew if you two could be friends."

"Wouldn't that cause problems for Jennifer with Alexis's father?" I asked.

"No, because it seems the guy Tony, who she claimed was the father, got a blood test and it's not his child, now she claims it's some ex-boyfriend that's locked up for the next few years."

"What happened to Da Rock? Why did they break up? At least then she didn't have to worry about getting pregnant."

"I don't know, Ed. It's not my concern. I just want what's best for the children."

"Alright, Mom. I'll call to speak with her and see what's going on."

Walking back to my unit after the visit, I contemplated the idea of being on good terms with Jennifer, deciding to give her a call.

"Hey Jennifer, how are you doing?"

"I'm good. How are you?" she answered sounding pleasantly surprised.

"I'm fine, just spent some time with my mom."

"Yeah, she told me she was going to see you. I'll get Drew."

"Hold up, Jennifer. I called to talk with you also."

"Oh, yeah?"

"Why is there a problem with that?"

"No, not at all. It's just surprising, what's up?"

"During the visit my mom said you mentioned possibly coming down to visit which surprised me."

"Yeah, I got the feeling you didn't want me to come."

"Nah, I don't think it's a good idea for Drew to see me here."

"I don't either, plus he's convinced you're in college, and when you graduate, you're taking him to Disney World."

"Yeah, I promised that. How's your daughter doing?"

"Oh, she's fine, beautiful and adores her brother."

"That's great, so I'll talk to my mother and the two of you can arrange a trip down."

"Ok, is it cool for me to write you?" she asked, which shocked me.

"Yeah and send some pictures."

"Are you going to write back?"

"Of course," I answered, amazed that she wanted to write me at all.

"Ok, let me get Drew."

As she placed the phone down, I was smiling to myself at the fact that I had a sane conversation with Jennifer after all these years. Hearing the movement of the phone on the other end, brought back my attention.

"Hey Daddy," said the all too familiar feminine voice of Drew.

"Hey Buddy! How you doing?"

"Good just outside playing, how's college?" he asked.

"It's good I've been studying hard. How are you doing in school?"

"Good, got a hundred on my math test," he stated with pride.

"Great job! I'm really proud of you."

"Thanks, Dad."

"I'm told you're a great big brother."

"Oh, Daddy my sister is just so adorable; she's the prettiest little thing. I just love her."

"Well, she's going to need a strong brother to watch after her growing up, can you handle it?"

"You know it, ain't no one messing with my little sister," he said.

The tone of his voice sounded just like he was one of Cece's crew members.

"Well, that's really good to know, you listen to your mother."

"Will do," he answered.

"I love you and miss your face."

"Love you too, Dad."

*

During the next few weeks, I received letters from Jennifer, explaining how she's never loved anyone like me, made foolish mistakes and how she couldn't wait to see me.

When she came down to visit, I have to admit, all eyes were on her as she strolled across the visitor's floor. Wearing a black, slim cut, tight dress, that accented her big hips and tiny waist, and a sexy white blouse with two buttons opened at the top, showing just enough cleavage to have one's mind running wild. The attention felt good as she came into my arms, and we hugged with an extra-long embrace.

I made sure to keep the conversation neutral by not touching on sensitive issues like Drew's behavior or her behavior for that matter. I know how defensive and explosive she could be and it was that last thing I needed in my life.

CHAPTER THIRTEEN

Re-establishing my criminal enterprise took no time. Within months I had my old customers back, plus a few new ones; workers moving weight and my connect showing he was happy that I was back, it was as if I never left.

Operating on an average of 4-5 hours of sleep, I still made sure to spend time with Drew. Some days it would be first thing in the morning since I was spending a night or two out of the week at their apartment.

My cell phone began to ring at 5:20 pm like clockwork showing Jennifer's number.

"Hey Eddie. I just got home and wanted to know what you're doing for dinner tonight?"

"We ate out the last two nights so why don't you cook and call me back when it's just about ready."

"Just come over now, I don't even know what I'm going to make yet."

"When you know call me."

"So just come now."

"I'm busy now."

"Busy doing what?" she asked.

"Busy doing none ya'."

"What the hell is none ya'?"

"None of ya' business!" I answered.

I laughed aloud, knowing it frustrated the shit out of her when I wouldn't answer her questions. I did it to keep clear boundaries so she knew we weren't in a committed relationship.

"Are you coming or not because I'm not calling again."

"I'll be there."

"When?"

"When I get there," I said, hanging up the phone making my point clear.

Trying to make eating dinner with Drew a habit also meant eating with Jennifer and Alexis, who was an added joy to the abnormality of the circumstances.

Treating Alexis, the same as Drew was the natural thing to do for me. When I brought Drew sneakers, I had a pair for Alexis. I would take them both to the movies, loading up her car seat in the back of my two door Lexus coupe with no problem. So that evening I reached into the pocket of my black leather jacket, I spoke to them both announcing that I had a surprise.

"What's the surprise, Daddy?" Drew asked with his eyebrows lifted high.

"Let's wait until your mother finishes serving the dinner."

"Mom, do you need some help?"

"No, calm down, Drew, I'm almost done. Go turn off the TV and put on my Mary J. CD. But not too loud!"

Drew raced to turn off the television, the low sounds of Mary's "Share My World" was contributing to the ambience of the excitement. Drew was back at the table catching his breath. The steam rose from the yellow Spanish rice on my plate, with the aroma of Adobo spices combined with the brown beans on top. Picking through the rice, taking out the green olives, Drew placed them on my plate knowing I loved the taste of them. Alexis sat in her high chair wearing a pink Barbie bib, drinking a red juice from her sippy cup. Jennifer finally sat down and all eyes were on me.

"Ok, what's the surprise?" Jennifer asked.

"Yeah, Dad tell us, what is it? You got me waiting, I'm so excited," Drew stated moving side to side filled with excitement.

"Yeah, Da-da, surprise," Alexis said giggling with a smile.

"Drew, remember one of the promises I made to you when I was in college?" I said leaning back, pulling out the envelope and passing it along the table for him to open.

"Is this what I think it is Daddy?"

"Open it and see," I told him.

I wasn't surprised that the waiter was a living Tinker Bell, who got extra flamboyant once he heard the way Drew talked.

I wanted to tell him off and shout "Stop talking to my son!!" but for the sake of our trip, I bit my lip and drowned my anger like a man... in vodka!

"Hope you'll enjoy a fabulous dinner with us tonight, what a beautiful family," the waiter said with a passive tone of voice as he passed out the brown leather menus. Drew joined in right on cue.

"Why, thank you, aren't we a beautiful family" batting his eyes, tilting his head as he spread his arms wide, hands open presenting us for display.

"Well, you're just the cutest little man, aren't ya'?" the waiter continued.

"Yes, I am," Drew replied.

"Wow, I like your confidence," the waiter answered.

"Can we order our drinks?" I cut in on what seemed to be like fairy flirting. "I'll take a vodka with cranberry juice, 2 cubes of ice, what type of sodas you two want?"

"Orange soda, Da-da," Alexis answered.

"I'll take a Coors's Light," Jennifer said.

"And for your, Mr. Confident?" the waiter asked.

"I'll take a Diet Coke."

"Diet?" I said getting unnerved.

"I'm trying to watch my figure, Daddy."

"Just bring him a regular Coke." I demanded tightening my fist, and catching myself ready to explode.

"That's a vodka with cran, 2 cubes of ice for Dad, a Coors Light for Mom, orange soda for the princess and a diet, no regular coke for Mr. Confident, be right back!"

With a wink and a twirl, Tinker Bell dashed off to get our drinks.

"Eddie, what's wrong with you?" Jennifer asked, scolding me with a piercing stare.

"What? There's nothing wrong?" I lied.

"You were a little moody with the waiter," she said.

"He was acting too friendly."

"He's supposed to be friendly dad. Do you want him to be mean?" Drew added.

Wait, I'm the one who planned this whole trip, why am I the bad guy? I thought.

"No, I just want him to take of our order and bring our food. I'm starving."

Mr. Jolly was right back passing out our drinks.

"Do we know what the glamorous family would like for dinner?" he asked, sounding just like a bitch.

"I'll take the salmon platter with rice and a Cesar salad," I said.

"Great choice, sir, the salmon is magnificent, and for your wife?"

"She's not my wife; I'm just her baby's daddy." Winking at Jennifer as I gulped down my drink.

"I'll take the cheese lasagna with a garden salad and a children's spaghetti for Alexis. Drew, what do you want? Jennifer asked.

Placing both elbows on the table, Drew rested his chin between both hands, sucking his teeth, head twisting, reading each item from the children's menu as if he didn't already know what he wanted to order.

He gets the chicken fingers and fries. This is nothing new, every time we go out he orders the same exact thing no matter what. Now it was like he was stalling, keeping the waiter there looking over his shoulder at the menu together.

"Drew, just order your... Before I..."

"Eddie!!"

The stone cold eyes of Jennifer gave me a look that brought back old memories. Finally finished with reading the menu Drew said, "I think I'll try the chicken fingers and fries."

"What a surprise" I threw up my arms in defeat. "Can you bring me another vodka?" I tried to stare down the waiter but he was just too gay to care.

"With cran and two cube of ice coming up!"

Drew being so comfortable with the waiter irked me. The waiter probably knew what it was to be a gay child and just did all he could, encouraging Drew to be comfortable with who he is. I didn't want Drew to be comfortable with being gay, he was already way too complacent with sounding and acting like a girl.

Their little friendly parley continued throughout the meal, but I ignored it and shot Drew a few dirty looks when his feminine waiter friend was lingering at the table too long, but he didn't care since his mother, the protector was there. Drew looked right back at me like I was crazy.

Although the food was delicious, the interaction between Drew and the waiter had me pissed and glad when the check finally arrived.

There was no reason to call back to argue, nothing I could say would make her happy, we both knew it. What I did say got the point across since she didn't ring my phone. Three days later on Tuesday night I called their apartment before picking up Drew.

"Hey-hey!" he answered.

"Drew, you want to grab something to eat?"

"Yeah, Dad," the excitement vibrating in his voice.

"Check if it's cool with your mom."

"Mom! My daddy's coming to take me to eat," he shouted.

In the background over the sounds of the television, I heard Jennifer's response.

"Fine, when?"

"It's cool dad, how long?"

"I'll be out front in ten minutes."

"I'll be ready."

Driving up to the house and beeping the horn, Drew bounded right out, pulling on his red Nike wind breaker, skipping each step, jogging to the passenger side and throwing himself in the front seat.

"What's up Drew?" he was all smiles as usual.

"Hey Daddy."

"Where you want to eat?"

"Where ever you want."

"Ok, how's school going?" I asked.

I pulled away and headed towards the local T.G.I.F. restaurant.

"Schools good, I got another hundred on my spelling test."

"That's excellent my man! What else's been going on?"

"Nothing much, Mommy has a new boyfriend."

"That was fast; at least it's a boy." A quick glimpse of "Da Rock" mentally made me smile saying "I hope he makes her happy. Do you like him?"

"Yeah, he seems cool, but I wish you two never broke up."

"Drew, we weren't together like that. Your mother and I are just good friends," I explained.

"She didn't sound like she was your friend dad."

"Why would you say that?"

"She said she hates you and you only care about yourself."

"Your mother is just upset, as long as I care about you, we have nothing to worry about," I answered.

"But Dad, don't you think it's better for everyone if you and Mom worked it out?"

"It wouldn't be better for me or her. She wants one thing in life and I want another, don't worry yourself about it," I said rubbing his head, making him smile as I pulled into the parking lot.

Stepping out of my gray Lexus, I could see the worried expression on Drew's face. The dream of living with both parents came to an end.

It bothered me knowing it upset Drew but there was no way I would commit my life to constant misery and drama just to make him happy. Selfish as it seems it's how I felt and I stuck to it.

After dinner when I pulled up to drop Drew off, Jennifer was outside inhaling a cancer stick, wrapped in the arms of her new victim, leaning against his purple Hyundai Sonata. Jerome was tall, with a dark completion, stick figure built, a straight corn ball that I knew from high school.

"You see, Drew, Mommy's already happy with her new boyfriend, and I'm happy being single. I'm picking you up on Friday to spend the weekend at Grams."

"Ok Dad," he said.

Leaning over for a hug and kiss goodbye, looking up, I saw Jennifer headed towards the car. "Hurry up, Drew, I don't want to talk to your... Jennifer, what's up?" I said as she reached my open window.

"You know it's your weekend to take Drew," she barked at me.

"Yes, I just told him to double check with you to make sure it's all right boss."

"Good because I am the boss!" she spat.

Taking a long drag from her Newport, she quickly blew out the smoke towards my face.

"Blow that shit over there, you know I hate the smell of smoke."

"I'll blow it where ever I want!"

"Ok, Jennifer, I'll be here to pick him up on Friday. I got to go."

"You rushing to fuck your other bitches?"

"No, I'm rushing to get fucked by my other bitches!" I flashed a big smile, put the Lexus in drive, pulling off as I waved to Drew at the top of the stairs. I turned up "Still Dre" from the Chronic CD, setting out to make some money for the night.

Not another word was said during the ride. I wasn't even mad at myself for yelling at Drew, feeling like that entire scene was a setup, showing me the type of behavior their pushing on him to get revenge somehow.

We're going to turn your son into a flaming queer! Jennifer and her family's voices were chanting in my head. *They're going to turn me away from my son.* What I thought to myself of course.

*

As soon as my Lexus rolled to a stop, Drew flung open the door, leaped out and whipped the door shut, with a defiant look before running into the house. I wanted to scream at the top of my lungs, but I bit my lip.

"Hey honey!" my mother greeted him.

"Hi, Grams."

"Come give me a hug, it keeps me young."

Embraced in her arms, rocking Drew side to side, she placed a kiss on top of his head as I walked in shutting the front door.

"Hi, Ed! Come keep your mother young and beautiful!"

Releasing Drew, she spread open her arms, embracing me in a hug. We both noticed Drew stomping his way up the stairs, slamming the door to his room.

"Something I should know about?" she asked.

Releasing from our embrace, pulling out the kitchen chair, she motioned me to take a seat.

"When I picked Drew up, I walked in to find him playing with a Barbie doll."

"Was he with his sister?"

"Alexis was nowhere in sight. Julie, Jennifer, and Kelly were all encouraging that shit like it's normal as hell."

"Did you say anything?"

"Yeah, and the 3 of them started in on me so I just walked out and waited in the car."

"Well, that was good on your part."

"Mom, I hoped while I was away, he would grow out of all the girly shit but it's gotten worse. I don't know what to do."

"You just have to be a loving father, let me fix some chamomile tea too help you relax."

Filling the kettle with water, she placed it on the white Kenwood stove, turning the dial on high.

"What you need to do is make a witch's brew that will get him to act normal."

"Witch's brew, huh? You've been talking to Peppy again?"

"No, he's afraid to be my friend because of you."

With a smile, she reached in the cherry wood cabinet pulling out two of her favorite mugs, placing them on the counter.

Sounds of Drew blasting the "Pussy Cat Dolls" came from his room, irking my nerves.

"Thank God Cindy Lauper was before his time, 'Girls Just Want to Have Fun' would have been his favorite song!"

After 5 minutes, the slow whistling of the kettle drew my mother to the stove. She poured the hot water and gently dipped the chamomile tea bags up and down as steam rose off the brims of the mugs.

"What are you planning to do with Drew this weekend?"

"Sign him up for ballerina lessons!"

"Ed!"

"I'm kidding, we'll probably see a movie or something."

The music got louder as Drew opened the door to his room and came down stairs.

"Grams, can I go over to Vinny's?"

"Don't you think you should ask me? I'm right here."

"You don't like the way I talk, so it doesn't make sense to ask you anything."

"What makes sense is showing some respect. The answer is no! Go back up in your room!"

"God!!" he yelled, stomping back up the stairs, and slamming his door.

"You see what I'm talking about?'

"Calm down, your both still upset. You going out tonight?'

"Yeah, if it's ok with you."

"Then go enjoy yourself. Tomorrow's a fresh new day."

I didn't wait for tomorrow. That night after downing a pair of Heinekens, the events with Drew were still fresh on my mind. Around 12:00 am before going home, I stopped at Hot Bagels.

"Drew, you awake?"

"Yeah."

"Come on in my room and eat while we watch some TV."

"Ok, Dad."

"I see you found plenty of things for Alexis and yourself," I said.

"Yeah, they have great deals; I can't wait to hit the other stores," she answered. After what seemed like forever, hardly moving any closer to the register, I got restless.

"Look this shit is crazy. I'm going to wait for you over at the front of the line."

"Fine."

"Come on, Drew."

"I want to stay with my mother."

Alexis was comfortable sitting in the seat on the cart, so I walked to the front of the store where they had a red cushioned couch I relaxed on and made a few calls. Thirty minutes later, Drew walked up.

"Dad, Mom's next at the register."

"Finally! It's been damn near an hour!"

At the front of the line we still had to wait another ten minutes until I finally got to do my part, which was pay the bill. *Kids' school clothes $400, $200 for Jennifer's clothes, one dress shirt for myself $50...getting out of this line...priceless* I thought as I paid for everything.

With 4 full bags of clothes we reached the Oldsmobile, loading them in the trunk, Jennifer was fueled up and ready to hit the next store.

"Let's go over to the Polo store, I know they have some nice stuff."

"Hold up, Jennifer," I said shaking my head no.

"What's wrong?" she asked frowning her eyebrows.

"We just spent an hour and a half in one store," I complained.

"So what?"

"This shit is too crowded."

"That's how it is!"

"Look the kids have outfits for the first few days, I would rather come back tomorrow or during the week when everyone is at work."

"But I have to work!" She shot back.

"And you can go to work; I'll take care of all the shopping."

"I want to do the shopping today!"

"Well, I'm not dealing with this madness any more, I'm done. Take me back to my car."

"I can't believe you, Eddie!"

"Believe it, kids...get in the car."

"But Dad you promised you would buy me lots of clothes," Drew whined.

"And I will, tomorrow when all the crowds are at work."

"Eddie, I planned on shopping all day!" Jennifer said with a scorching tone.

"Me too, but this isn't shopping, it's stand in line all day. Let's go!"

"I can't believe you had me drive all the way out here to go to one store!"

"You got some clothes and a full tank of gas. I've spent over $600 so stop complaining." I said, closing the passenger door.

Staring ahead leaning on the armrest in the middle of the seat, I felt Drew's foot kick the back of the arm rest hitting my elbow.

"Drew, stop kicking the seat."

Two more kicks later caused me to turn my head, looking him straight in the eyes.

"I said stop kicking the seat, you're hitting my arm."

Ten seconds past when he thrust both his feet against the back of the arm rest hitting my elbow with the heels of his sneakers. Spinning around, raising up over the front seat... I punched Drew in the center of his chest.

The shock on his face registered as he took a deep breath then let out a shrieking cry.

"Ahhh, I can't breathe!!"

"Oh my God!!" Jennifer shouted as she pulled the Oldsmobile over onto the shoulder of the road, hoping out, ripping open the back passenger door, checking Drew's chest as if he got shot by a rifle.

"Here we go," I said aloud to myself.

"I can't believe you punched my son!" she yelled.

"I tapped his chest, he didn't want to listen."

"You shouldn't put your hands on him!" she shouted.

"Jennifer, you slap and hit him all the time, I'm not trying to hear your mouth or his!"

Drew cried for another 5 minutes and finally calmed down. I pulled the punch, knowing that I hardly touched him, but the dramatics between Drew and his mother were at an all-time high. The fact that it was the first time I hit Drew is what had him so shocked, especially in the presence of his almighty protector.

I didn't say a word for the remainder of the ride back. Staring straight ahead counting each exit until we reached the one leading to their house. Pulling into her driveway I told Drew, "I'll pick you up tomorrow after school to finish shopping."

"Ok, Dad," he replied.

Jennifer gave an evil stare as I walked to my Lexus and left.

*

Sprinting out the apartment, Drew skipped down every other step, dashing for the passenger side door grinning ear to ear as he climbed in.

"Hi, Daddy!"

"Hey! How was your first day of school?"

"It was good."

"You like your teacher?"

"Yeah, she's cool," he answered.

"Well, you look real cool in those sharp new clothes. Let's go finish shopping."

Another clear bright day with just the two of us in the Lexus sports coupe, warm rays fell through the open sun roof, the breeze hit us just right, Drew was bopping along to Jay-Z's "Big Pimping." I turned down the volume as he was singing along... It put a smile on my face.

"Dad, that's my song!"

"What you know about big pimping?"

"I love the beat, it's slamming," he answered.

"I'll start it over after we talk," I said.

"About what?"

"Yesterday."

"Oh, when you got Mommy pissed."

"Your mother's always pissed. I'm talking about you kicking my elbows and not listening after I told you to stop more than once," I said looking him straight in the eyes.

"No matter what I did, you shouldn't hit me."

"Hold on, no matter what I tell you, you need to listen. I'm your father."

"Uh, huh," he mumbled.

"Have I ever hit you before?" I asked.

"No."

"I surprised you right?"

"Yeah."

"You surprised me with your disrespect which I won't put up with at any time. I don't care if your mother's there or not, you understand me?" his eyes looked sincere as he answered.

"Yeah Dad."

"I'm sorry I hit you," I admitted.

"It's all right but Mommy says she doesn't trust you with me now."

"She said that?" I glanced at him while keeping my eyes on the road.

"Yep!"

"So why are you with me now?"

"I don't know."

"I'll deal with your mom, don't worry, turn up the music."

I jumped into the H.O.V. lane, pushing the speedometer to 80, blaring the speakers as we rapped along with the favorite parts of the song together. Drew put the CD on repeat for the entire ride to the outlet.

All the stores were empty, and we zipped right through grabbing sneakers, sweatshirts, pants, shorts, jackets, and shirts. We had different shopping bags in every hand stuffed with clothes for Drew and Alexis and we filled the trunk and back seat. We were in good spirits stuffing it all in, and I knew the $2,500 dropped on this shopping spree was enough clothes for the rest of the year.

"Good job, Dad! Alexis is going to love what you brought her." I smirked at my son's happiness and wanted to extend our day.

"Let's eat before I drop you off."

"Ok"

As we were waiting for the check, my cell phone rang.

"Hello?"

"How much longer until you bring my son home?"

"Not long Jennifer we're almost there."

"Where is he?"

"Hold on," I said passing Drew the phone.

"Hello," he answered then said, "We just finished eating at the diner." And then a quick, "Okay, bye."

Snapping the phone shut Drew passed it back to me. I slid it into the side pocket of my Nike jacket.

"What was that about?" I asked him

"She's checking to see if I'm all right."

"If you're all right?" I said thinking to myself, *this bitch is really bugging out, making an issue over nothing.*

"Yeah."

Pulling up to the house I popped the trunk and filled as many bags as Drew could carry. I grabbed the rest. Jennifer, Alexis and Drew were in the bedroom going through the bags he carried up.

"Drew, here's the rest for you and Alexis, I have to go. I'll call you." I said sticking my head in the front door where I placed the rest of the bags.

"Ok, Dad. Thanks!" Drew yelled.

"Thanks, Da-da," Alexis waddled towards the door giving me a wave good-bye and I waved back.

Two days later I called Drew.

"Hello?" Jennifer answered.

"Hey! Is Drew there, I was calling to see if he wanted to grab a bite to eat."

"Eddie, I'm not too comfortable with Drew being alone with you right now."

"Really." I said.

"Yeah...really."

"And why's that?"

"Because you hit him!" she barked.

"Well, he was being disrespectful, and why did you let him go shopping with me if you're oh so worried?"

"Believe me… I almost didn't," she replied.

"Look, I don't have time for your drama, if you want to act like a crazy bitch do that."

"You haven't seen crazy, mother fucker! And you won't see my son until I feel I can trust you with him."

"Hey Jennifer..."

"What?"

Click.

CHAPTER SEVENTEEN

"Bleep"- my Nextel chirped.

"A-yo!"

"Bleep"

"What's up?"

"Bleep"

"There's a little problem, the safe's in the floor so it's going to take longer than expected."

"Bleep"

"All clear out here, nothing from Ray so do what you got to do to get it done."

I was watching the Jiffy Lube from across the street, behind the wheel of an Explorer that I literally "borrowed" off the lot an hour earlier. Plastic covered the seats, and the price tag sticker on the passenger side window with a dealer's license plate was purposely left on so we can report it stolen should anything go wrong.

If things go according to plan, I'll just drop off Joe and his goombahs, return the truck and enjoy a nice pay day. Keeping my eyes peeled for trouble, while working the radios with our other line of security was my main responsibility and part in this heist. Our other safeguard was Ray, a Suffolk County crooked cop out of the third prescient, who we had on the payroll, was parked in a silver B.M.W about a mile up the road monitoring his police scanner.

"Bleep"

"Yeah Buddy."

"Bleep"

"Ray, there's going to be a little delay, this one's in the floor."

"Bleep"

"Ok."

At first I was a little hesitant when Joe asked me to work with his crew doing scores. He was a customer that brought a lot of weight before I did time in Virginia. When we re-connected, he changed his hustle to doing "Licks" and other jobs from his connections with the Colombo crime family. Joe was a John Gotti want-to-be since the day we met. With his new house and three tanning salons, it appeared that crime does pay.

"Bleep"

"Yo! there's a red Mustang pulling in."

"Bleep"

"Who is it?"

"Bleep"

"Don't know, looks like they're turning around, just stay out of sight."

The unexpected vehicle paused shinning its high beam lights towards the glass garage doors.

"Bleep"

"Ray, you hear anything?"

"Bleep"

"Nope, all clear."

"Bleep"

"Be on point, we have an unknown guest."

"Bleep"

"Got cha."

"Bleep"

"Yo! Come get us we're getting out of here!"

"Bleep"

"Joe, calm down, it's probably nothing. They're pulling out now."

"Bleep"

"Ed."

"Bleep"

"Yeah, Ray?"

"Just heard the call. Someone saw them."

"Bleep"

"I'm on it."

"Bleep"

"Spots been blown, I'm on the way!"

I turned the key, slammed the shift in drive and punched the gas.

The Explorer took off, rubber biting the concrete launching forward. I pulled up still rolling, as three doors opened with Joe and the rest of his crew diving in head first.

"What the fuck, guy?" Joe managed to get out between panting ...

"A good Samaritan called it in."

"Damn, we were just about to pull it out, fucking floor safes!" he shouted.

Zipping away at first to lose any potential tails, I slowed down and merged with traffic once I felt we were safe.

"Look here they come." I warned watching 3 police cars with flashing blue and red lights wiz by us towards the Jiffy Lube.

"Bye, ass holes!" I said waving my hand with a smile as they passed.

"Fucking, clowns" Joe said. "We just about had it."

"Joe, they just about had us, be glad for that." I reminded him.

"You're right."

"Bleep"

"You guys clear?" Ray asked.

"Bleep"

"Yeah, headed towards the house."

"Bleep"

"Meet you there."

Joe's house was in an upscale neighborhood in St. James. An assistant district attorney and Suffolk County's top cop lived on the same block just a few houses down. Inside the garage we all sipped cold bottles of Heinekens, laughing off the close call of the night.

"There goes my Cancun money," Ray bitched.

"Yeah right, you're still good from the King Kullen job; easiest 50 G's you ever made." Joe joked.

"And the fastest I ever spent," Ray replied.

"That's your fault. Anyway, my guy has plenty of jobs lined up so be ready, you'll have your Cancun money."

We finished our drinks and Joe followed me in his black Cadillac Seville to return the Explorer to the Ford lot up the street. Making a right on the side block that ran parallel to the huge Ford dealership, I parked in the exact spot from where I took it two hours before, the only difference being the miles on the speedometer.

Removing the dealer plate, I tucked it under my black Polo jacket, walking to where Joe was waiting. With things set back to normal with the Explorer I had him bring me to my Lexus.

"Changing the radio station from Z-100 to hot 97, Jay-Z's "I'm a Hustler" came over the speaker. Pulling up to my ride, Joe turned the radio off.

"What's up with that thing you mentioned?" he asked.

"With the security guard?"

"Yeah."

"I'm looking into it."

"Let's get that done, sounds like a nice pay day," Joe said.

"If it checks out I'll know next week."

"My guy called and wants to meet you."

"For what?"

"He's into your other business, and I told him I'm done with that."

"Call me between 5-5:30 tomorrow, we'll all meet up," I said.

*

The following day when my phone rang at quarter past five, it wasn't who I expected.

"Hello?"

"Eddie, It's Jennifer."

"No kidding, what's up?"

"You need to come over to talk with Drew," she demanded.

"I'm a little busy, put him on the phone."

"He had a problem at school; he's upset so you need to come over here."

"What happened," I asked, now very concerned.

"If you care you'll come and tell the bitch you're busy with you'll see her later!"

"You're the only bitch I'm busy with so I guess I'll see you later; tell me what's going on."

"When are you coming?'

"I'm turning around now."

"Then I'll let him tell you."

Click.

My green Ford Taurus with dark tint was my work car that I was driving, since earlier that day I was in the city taking care of business with my contact. Ten minutes after talking with Jennifer my phone rang again.

"A-Yo! Eddie, my brother, how you doing?"

"I'm good, Joe."

"Great, I'm here with the friend of mine who's really looking forward to meeting you, he's heard good things. How long until you're here?"

"Something just came up with my son, let me call you back in a couple of minutes."

"A-Yo, guy, this is a very important man, don't make me look bad."

"A-Yo Joe, this is my son, I'll call you as soon as I'm done, ok Gumba, Bada Bing, bada boom, and all that good stuff."

"You're a real funny guy you know that," he said.

"It's what I do, I'll hit you back as soon as I'm done."

I approached the side steps leading up to their apartment, wondering what could have happened that she couldn't tell me over the phone.

Cigarette smoke hung in the air like a fog, attaching to my clothes and invading my lungs. Three light knocks and little movements of the knob exhibited Alexis attempt at letting me in.

The silhouette of Jennifer approached and the door opened with Alexis smiling face, her arms shot out stretching, I bent down to lift her. She was all smiles and love.

"Hey baby girl."

"Da-da."

"How's everyone doing?" I asked walking into the living room.

"We're fine, Drew's in the bedroom."

"Ok, right to business I see," I said walking towards the back room.

"Alexis, watch TV while we talk with Drew."

Entering the bedroom, I expected a black eye or fat lip on Drew since he was laying on his bed in the dark. I flicked on the light and saw he looked perfectly fine.

"What's up, Drew?"

"Hey Dad," his soft-spoken voice hid sadness.

"Sit up, Drew, tell your father what's the matter," Jennifer commanded.

"Easy, Jennifer, damn calm down; Drew what happened?" I asked.

Sitting close, pulling him near me, nudging his rib cage to make him crack a smile, he did and began to talk. "A bunch of kids at school were making fun of me today."

"Making fun of you how?" I asked.

"They were saying I talked like a girl."

"Eddie, we have a problem!" Chris shouted when I answered my Nextel.

"What's up!!"

"Erick got thrown out of a window from the top floor of the building he was in by some jealous boyfriend!"

"Say no more, call me when you know how he is."

To take a quote from the rapper Nas...

"Sometimes the rap game is just like the crack game."

Within 20 minutes, I was on my way to Jersey in my green Taurus with 3 of my street soldiers, a black duffel bag in the trunk with hoodies, 4 pairs of gloves, a throw away license plate, and enough metal to get us 10 years for felons in possession. As we were crossing the George Washington Bridge leaving New York into New Jersey, my phone chirped from Chris again.

"I got some good news and bad news," Chris said.

"Is Erick going to make it?"

"That's the good news, but he's fucked up."

"Whoever's responsible is going to be fucked up; we're already in Jersey."

"That takes me to the bad news, there's no boyfriend so call off the hounds."

"What?" I asked completely confused.

"Yeah, there wasn't any boyfriend... Erick jumped out the window."

"Get the fuck out of here!!"

"Crazy right? He tried to kill himself," Chris said.

"He was fine at the video shoot," I said.

"Well, who knows what he was thinking."

"Alright Chris, I'll talk to you back in Long Island."

After an official investigation, the girlfriend revealed that Erick acted normal as usual when he arrived at her apartment. He told her he was going to take a nap after the seemingly endless video shoot. Minutes later she went and peeked inside the room to see an empty bed and open window which she looked out of seeing Erick was face down in a pool of blood on the sidewalk below, no sound, no scream, no warning. Just a quiet suicide leap from a bedroom window with what seemed to be no cause.

Naturally, I was shocked. Erick appeared to be on top of the world. I personally turned down shows for $25,000 as he was booked. Erick had just inked a huge deal with J-records, so looking from the outside, life couldn't have been better.

The rumors of him being gay were nothing new. I didn't think it was affecting him to the degree that he wanted to kill himself. Now this attempted suicide added fuel to the fire, causing even more of a stir in the media.

After a few weeks, Erick was back in the studio working and doing interviews promoting his album. When asked questions pertaining to what made him want to kill himself, Erick professionally laughed it off and replied.

"That's between me and my creator."

No matter how much the interviewer pushed, Erick just stuck to the script, moving on to the business of music.

*

Homosexuality and the entertainment industry is a culture that go hand and hand, like in prison. Promoters of the hottest clubs, the best stylists, Artists and Repertoire (A&R's) of the record labels and executives of every aspect of the entertainment industry have homosexuals in powerful positions.

If the gay and lesbian community has a reason to black ball your record, club, clothing line, or whatever you're involved in, it could be done as easy as 1, 2, 3. They're like a secret society, stronger than the illuminati or Masons.

When the rapper Eminem said something offensive towards the homosexual community, he felt the pressure their society wields. At the next major award show, Eminem performed with and at the end embraced Elton John as a sign of reconciliation.

The music industry is the perfect example of how meaningless one's sexual preference is. If the way a musician acts in their private life was the determining factor to whether or not I enjoyed a song, I wouldn't be able to listen to any music.

It was easy for me to apply my all accepting attitude in the entertainment world, but on the home front, when it was my son, there's just a big "Something" that made it harder for me to support. Numerous times I've been asked if Erick was gay, and I've answered that I never personally saw anything that would make me comfortable with saying, "Yes! Erick is gay!"

Erick ignored the topic, even when he had the perfect opportunity to address it with the person who was said to have first reported that he was gay to the public years before.

Wendy Williams had one of the biggest radio talk shows on 103.5 in New York City. I was told the rumor started years earlier when Wendy and Erick had an intimate relationship. At the time Wendy first had her radio show on Hot 97.

After spending the night at Erick's on Long Island, Wendy asked him to order a town car to take her to work in time for her radio show. Erick told Wendy to take the Long Island Rail Road and an argument ensued.

Wendy was described as a crazy infatuated groupie with her feelings hurt, leaving Erick's house as a woman scorned. The next thing you know, Wendy's on her radio show proclaiming Erick as the gay rapper.

To my ears, the story sounded farfetched, but I've heard stranger tales. Greg Taylor who told me this, is another close friend of Erick's who was around him during this time, so I didn't see any reason for him to lie to me.

Accepting the story, I felt like it was time to confront it and set the record straight.

Erick was booked doing radio shows and interviews from early morning until late night promoting the release of his new album. As we rode in the back of a black Lincoln truck, I told the driver to head to the offices of 103.5.

"Erick, we're booked at the Wendy Williams show in 30 minutes."

"I'm not doing her show," he replied non-nonchalantly.

"Why not?" I asked already knowing the reason.

"You know she's the one that started that rumor."

"And, what better place to address it. All of New York is listening, call her on her bull shit live on the air!"

"That bitch damn near ruined my career, I'm not doing her show!" he aggressively stated.

It was the first and only time Erick ever raised his voice towards me. After a slight pause of awkward silence, I said, "Ok, no Wendy, fuck that bitch!"

*

The topic of the gay rumor came up between us one other time when we took a trip to Atlanta.

The first place Erick wanted to go was to visit Divine, who's tall, dark skinned with a slim built and a talented dancer, making him one of the top choreographers in the music industry. He's worked with Jennifer Lopez, Puffy, Usher, and Beyoncé. I knew of Divine at the time but had yet to meet him.

Pulling up to an enormous townhouse in a gated community that had exotic automobiles parked in every driveway, hinted to just how much a top choreographer makes.

Wide gray stone steps lead to the front glass door, that quickly opened after Erick pushed the circular button, sounding the musical chimes inside.

"Heeeey, Erick Sermon, welcome, welcome!"

The flamboyancy of Divine's mannerisms didn't go unnoticed. Being a male choreographer who teaches the most beautiful women how to move and look sexy in music videos, I wasn't surprised that he was a little feminine.

"Divine, this is Eddie."

"Nice to meet you, please come in and make yourself at home," Divine greeted.

"Nice to meet you, too," I said walking inside, looking up at the impressive vaulted ceiling. Following behind Erick, Divine lead us to a flight of stairs that proceeded down to the studio in his basement.

"The people from Universal will be here any minute to meet and hear Akon perform, I finally think I got him a deal."

"Akon's my man," Erick said as we reached the bottom stairs into a state of the art recording studio. Akon along with his band of three musicians were rehearsing. The music stopped once we entered.

"Erick Sermon!! What an honor!" Akon shouted. "This is a sign that I'm getting that deal with Universal!" he continued, dressed in designer jeans, red color shirt and white Nikes.

"They'll be the lucky ones, you've been overlooked for too long," Erick said, then introducing me, "You remember Eddie."

"Of course, how you been?" Akon asked.

"Good yourself?" I replied.

"A little nervous but better now that the green-eye bandit is in the house!" Nodding his head and clapping his hands.

The chime of the doorbell caused Divine to spin around and sprint back up the stairs, returning with four staff members from Universal records. Akon performed his single "Locked Up" and it was all claps and congratulations once he was done.

"Divine, call me when you're done with business and we'll get up."

"Ok Erick, it won't be too long."

For the next 4 days in Atlanta, every time we would go to a restaurant, studio, or club, Divine would end up meeting Erick there. Magic City, the hottest strip club in Atlanta was our last stop, the night before we were set to leave on our early morning flight and Divine showed up there also.

Exotic women filled the club wearing nothing but G-strings and shiny tassels covering the tips of their nipples. This city wasn't Magic, it was heaven!

"Let me get a bottle of Grey Goose, a double shot of Hennessy, and 500 singles." I shouted to the bar tender over little John's "Yeah!!" exploding through the speaker.

Erick and Divine were off to the side talking with 2 girls they knew, while I was posted up at a table next to the dance floor with five big-butt, huge-breasted beautiful girls, drinking and having a good time. I was making it rain throwing cash without a care in the world.

With ass clapping, booties shaking, titties bouncing all in my face, I intuitively felt someone staring at me. Instinctively looking for the source, I gazed over my shoulder and saw that Divine had me locked in the cross hairs of his "Gaydar."

Quickly I turned back my attention to the naked women I was engulfed with, pulling them close, creating a protective shield surrounding me-but I still felt him gawking at me. Ignoring him completely so there doesn't become a situation, I was back partying with a sexy Dominican chick whose radar I was happy to be on.

After 45 minutes, just as I ordered a second bottle of Grey Goose, Erick grabbed my shoulder, spinning me around.

"Yo! We're ready to leave," he said.

"Leave? I got another bottle on the way, the nights just getting started," I said hollering over the music.

"I told Divine you would say something like that."

"You already know!"

"You good with a cab?"

"Yeah, I'm good, you taking those chicks?" I asked nodding in their direction.

"Nah, I'm going to drop off Divine and hit the hotel."

"Well, I'm going to be in the special care of this lady right here so don't wait up!" I said smiling in the eyes of this Latin goddess, while passing Erick the keys as I was being pulled away to continue the party.

The following morning, I was so hung over that Erick had to drive to the airport.

"What time did you go to sleep?" he asked as I leaned my head back with my eyes closed.

"I didn't. Me and that Dominican Mommy went to Waffle house, got back to the hotel and did the damn thing until you rang the room. She was still in the room when I left!"

" Ok Ed, A.T.L. treating you right."

"Yes, it has!" I said with a smile then continued. "But E, you ever think that the rumors of you being gay might stem from always hanging around your man?"

"Who Divine?"

"Yeah, who else? I mean he's cool and all but there's defiantly some extra scoops of sugar in his tank."

"Everybody knows Divine, that's just the way he is. You want to meet the hottest women in Atlanta, he's who you want to be around," Erick explained.

"Meeting beautiful women has never been a problem, Erick. If you want to stomp out this rumor, running around Atlanta with a flamboyant choreographer isn't really helping. I'm just saying."

"You're overreacting."

"Am I? Last night you left one of the most popular strip clubs with a fruity looking man and no bitches!"

"So?"

"So? For a person on the outside, who knows nothing about who Divine is and how long you've been friends, they might think that he was your boyfriend, assuming that the rumor is true!" I shot back.

"Nah, you worrying too much," he responded.

"I get paid to worry, if you want to dead the rumor, you have to be conscious of who you're seen with in the public's eye."

Erick just gave his uncomfortable laugh as I've seen him do during interviews. I expressed what was on my mind and said no more about it.

As I heard him close the door behind us, I walked down the stairs wondering how in the hell Jennifer knew about Maria and our apartment in Rhode Island.

*

Last July, I went with my man Gee to pick up some big money owed for some weed fronted to his cousin Wagner in Rhode Island. Normally the payment would be delivered, but since Gee had just purchased a platinum colored S-Class Mercedes, he was in the mood for a road trip.

After picking up the cash, we stopped at a local restaurant in Providence called Loco Pollo.

"Gee, the food is great but why don't they sell beers?" I asked.

"They probably lost their liquor license, go grab some Heinekens out the cooler in the Benz," he said.

"Yeah this Sprite ain't working, I'll be back." I said walking out the restaurant door headed towards the car when I shouted "Yo!! You're going to hit the curb!"

Breaks screeched as a green Honda's bottom front bumper scratched the concrete, right out front. I noticed the beautiful young driver flashing extra-long lashes in my direction. Spinning around, I back tracked as the passenger door opened and another beautiful Latin girl stepped out, walking into the restaurant.

"How you doing today?" I asked the driver.

"I'm fine."

"Yes you are, and I have to know the name of my future wife," I said flashing a smile.

"I'm Maria," she answered through a big smile of her own.

She turned her attention to the back seat, where her daughter was seated, with big brown eyes and her mother's lashes, she had dropped a bottle.

"And this little princess must be your daughter."

"Yes she is."

"Gorgeous just like her mother and what's her name?' I asked.

Blushing now she answered, "Her name's Alexis."

I immediately thought *'How ironic'* in regards to this little ones' name but Maria's sensuous voice with a heavy accent, rolling her "r's" and exquisite face cast a spell on me. Her DD sized breast busting out of the top of her shirt kept me mesmerized, until Gee stuck his head out from the door of the restaurant saying, "Where's the beers?"

"On the way! My wife's friend is placing their order, put it on my bill."

"Your wife, huh? This guy," he said shaking his head, turning to go back inside.

"I hope you'll let me take you out to a real dinner tonight." I asked.

Conversation with small talk continued until her friend came out with 2 bags. She thanked me for buying them lunch, and we exchanged cell phone numbers before she left. Grabbing two Heinekens, I went to finish the rest of my meal.

"I guess we're not leaving today," Gee stated.

"Nope."

For the rest of July and August, I was either in Rhode Island or Maria was in Long Island. In September, I rented a two-bedroom apartment at a building that used to be a fire house in the Federal Hill section of Providence.

The Neighborhood was a quiet residential area, the local restaurants served good food and we lived close enough to the highway that I could be at the airport within ten minutes.

South West Airlines had a local shuttle from Rhode Island to Long Island's Islip airport costing $50 for a 15-minute flight that ran on the hour from 7 am to 7 pm; it was perfect. In the mornings I'd be cooking breakfast for Maria, then seeing her off to college as if I was going to spend the day at home, lounging around watching movies.

"Bam!!"

Racing to the airport, I normally caught the 9:00 am flight. By 9:30 am, I was slamming the door to the Taurus speeding towards the city, then back to Long Island running around non-stop so I can catch the final return flight back to Rhode Island at 7:00 pm.

By 7:30 pm I was back in the apartment like I never left. Maria worked at Filene's Basement after school until 7:30 pm and then picked up Alexis from her grandmother's, walking in the door a little before 8:00 pm finding me in the bedroom watching the TV as if I never left.

There was only one other person that knew about the apartment and that I was living with Maria in Rhode Island... Gee!

CHAPTER TWENTY-ONE

The back and forth between Rhode Island and Long Island lasted for 6 months. Maria, Alexis, and I moved into a two-bedroom apartment in a complex in the Holbrook area of Suffolk, ten minutes away from my mother's house.

Maria met Drew on her previous visits to Long Island. Prior to their meeting I warned her...

"Drew is my son, I love him but his mother has him thinking he's a girl."

Although I had numerous girlfriends in the time since I came home from prison, Maria was the only one I introduced to Drew.

"Drew, this is Maria, my girlfriend I spoke to you about," he gave me a crazy eye kid's look saying:

Yeah, Dad, I kind of figured that out!

"Hi, Drew, I've heard a lot about you," Maria spoke sincerely to him.

"Hello. Hey Dad," he spoke as low as he could. "I like the way she talks."

"Drew, she can still hear you," I said smiling.

Maria blushed, embarrassed by her accent.

"She's from Columbia, English is her second language," I told him.

"OH! That's cool."

"How old are you, Drew?" she squatted down to his eye level.

"Eleven," he answered.

"You know Maria never had French toast until I made her some."

"Girl," Drew snapped. "You never had French toast? Even I know how to make it, I love French toast!" he spoke proudly.

"I do too, when your dad makes it for me."

She threw me her "approving bedroom eyes" look, thinking about the last time we woke up together and ate French toast.

The two of them hit it off from the start, which made it easier for me. The following morning Drew came into my room at my mother's house, while we were still sleeping.

"Maria," he whispered.

"Yes?" she whispered back.

"It's time to get up, I made you French toast."

"You did?"

"Yeah, and it tastes better than my dad's!" he said proud of himself.

"Ok, we'll be right down," she told Drew who happily scampered out of the room back down the stairs.

Coming up from behind Maria, I wrapped her in my arms as the cover fell to the floor. I placed my chin on her shoulder giving her a quick kiss saying, "He really likes you, he's never cooked for me, maybe he has a crush on you."

Maria turned around in my arms spinning her smile in my face asking, "Are you jealous?" as she wrapped her arms around my neck.

"Jealous? No, Maria, not jealous," giving her my playful smile. "Relieved."

We got dressed and found Drew wearing his grandmother's "Kiss the cook" apron. The table was set with matching plates, silverware, and glasses full of orange juice.

"Look at all this!" I said pulling out Maria's chair as she took a seat.

"What, Dad, it's breakfast" acting as if he did this every morning.

"You never made breakfast for me Drew."

"Well when Maria said she loved French toast, I wanted to show her that I can make it."

"You did this all by yourself?" she asked.

"Yeah, I've been cooking for years."

"I'm going to put on some coffee," I said.

By dinner time, Drew finished his scouting around the resort, returning with a sincere smile on his face, relaxed, and from the tone of his voice, back to normal.

"Dad, there are a lot of kids my age here and at the lake, it's so cool, they have paddle boats we can go on!" It was nice to see his change in spirit

"Ok, we can do that tomorrow," I encouraged.

"They have a big arcade downstairs in the basement too with all the cool games like street fighter, driving games, the old game you like Mrs. Pac-man and..."

"Did you see any horses?' I asked feeding his good mood and excitement.

"Yeah! Brown and white ones, too big for Alexa to ride so I don't know what you're going to do with her."

"They have smaller ponies for little kids her size. "We'll be fine," I told him.

*

The lights were movie-theater dim walking into the game room with flashing screens in all colors of the rainbow showing different arcade characters, space ships, and monsters doing battle with the kids that controlled the joysticks. The games played all the catchy anthems of the classic games I grew up playing, reminding me of all my younger years, feeding those machines quarters every chance I got. My eyes watched Donkey Kong standing at the top of his video world, throwing down barrel after barrel rolling zig-zag down the screen to that famous Donkey Kong theme song.

"Come on, Dad," Drew tugged my hand pulling me out of my moment of youth, toward all the newer games which ate up $20 in under an hour.

"I need more quarters, Dad," Drew asked.

Looking at my Rolex it was time to catch the hay ride.

"Come on, Drew, lets head out and check out the hay ride..."

"Dad, I don't want to go on that."

"Why not? It will be fun!"

"Fun for you and Maria maybe."

"You'll like it too-don't spoil the party."

"I want to play more games and hang out with kids my age," he whined typical for boys his age.

"Alright, Drew, if that's what you want," I said stuffing my hand into my front pocket pulling up a thick roll of mostly larger bills, his eyes lit up knowing I was caving in.

"Look, here's $20, make it last and be back to the room by 9:30 please."

"Thanks, Dad," he snatched the $20 turned and ran off into the sounds, and lights of video arcade fun. *As long as he's having a good time, was all that matters*, I thought.

Showing up for the hay ride without Drew got me two things, the first that freshly cut hay smell that reminded me of the country, and second, an ear full from Maria.

She gave me her unhappy look saying, "He didn't come because of us," she accused.

"That's not why, he liked the arcade and wanted to..."

"Yes it is!" she cut me off adding, "he's never acted so cold with me, I can tell you just don't want to admit it."

"No, I don't because I want to enjoy this vacation." I said bouncing Alexa up and down on a bale of hay, waiting in the back of this old-fashion style wooded wagon for other riders to climb aboard.

"Well, I can't enjoy it with him acting like that towards me and my daughter."

"He's not acting any way; he's just doing his own thing."

I didn't want Maria to feel bad but what she said was true-Drew was definitely moody around her and Alexa, but I knew any kid thrown into a new situation takes time to get acclimated.

The following day after a lazy breakfast, we took Drew up on his suggestion to ride the yellow two-seater paddleboats. With orange life vests on, Drew and I paddled out to the middle of the lake as fast as we could.

Having a little solo time with Drew felt good, with our legs burning from exhaustion, the hot sun melting our heads, we got out as fast as we could and just stopped peddling, watching others in paddleboats and drifting in a straight course on our wake.

I took advantage of this opportunity.

"Drew, you know the main reason I planned this trip was so we could all do things together and you keep dodging our quality time together," I told him.

"We're together now, Dad," he looked at me avoiding the point he knew I was getting at.

"Me and you are together because only two of us can come on this boat, which is cool because I love spending time with you, but I want you to spend time with all of us."

"Dad, why couldn't just you and I come here alone?"

"All right, I love you and miss you like crazy you know that right?"

"I know, and I love you Dad," he replied.

"Is your mother around?"

"Yeah, hold on." he told me before calling aloud for Jennifer. "Mom, Dad's on the phone!"

I was going to voice my concerns to his mother, even though she was a tough person to get to see common sense and to deal with. I understand she had childhood trauma that shapes the way she thinks, and I feel bad about it, I do, but that shit can only go so far. She's a real Ice queen to deal with, and I had a feeling this was going to be one of those times.

Pouring myself a shot of liquid courage and placing the new bottle of Grey Goose on the counter where Maria had it, I tossed back my shot just as the queen of mean said, "Hello?'

"I just wanted to check to see if the transitions going all right." I poured another shot and left it sitting as my fingers spun the shot glass slowly as my eyes stared at the clear vodka calling my name...Jennifer has this effect on me.

"Oh, it's fine. We should have come down when I first mentioned moving."

"Drew told me he's enjoying it so far, but I'm wondering if the kids are picking up on his strong New York accent as Drew likes to call it," I explained, trying to make my point without activating Jennifer's crazy bitch button.

"Why would they?" she asked oblivious or baiting me into an argument. I always had to break things down like talking to a three-year-old to her in my explanations and this conversation was no different.

"Jennifer, we both know kids can be cruel with him still talking like Shirley Temple and it's going to create problems, similar to what happened at his last school." Private thoughts flooded my mind, *I didn't call to argue, so don't activate her crazy bitch button - don't activate her crazy bitch button - whatever I do don't...*

"And that's why it was better to move down here, kids don't act like that in North Carolina!" her voice was getting progressively louder with each response, and increasing by the word.

"Kids act the same everywhere Jennifer," I reminded her in a still cool, controlled voice trying to have an actual parent-to-parent conversation about Drew and not activate her.

"Eddie!" she screamed in her I hate you devil voice.

...Crazy bitch button, too late.

"I'm down here; I would know! Drew is fine." You're so worried about how he talks, thinking he's gay, but he has plenty of girlfriends," she spat into the phone. And when women do this, there is only one thing all men are left to do to combat the crazy bitch button once it's pushed...

Toss back a shot of the hardest alcohol on hand, close your eyes and take a deep breath feeling the liquid lifeline crawl down into your belly and place the shot glass back on the table before you smash it into the wall, which is exactly what I did, before speaking deliberately and loudly back at crazy lady.

"He's 11 going on 12, he should be playing with boys his age, not liking them the way girls do!" I got louder excessively louder.

"Do sports!! Play with boys - not girls!!"

She spat right back, firing into the phone.

"You're just so homo-fucking-phobic that you're the one who's acting like a little bitch!!"

I gripped the phone so hard hearing that last remark of ignorance I almost broke it screaming.

"Now I'm acting like a bitch? Ok, Jennifer, you handle it!"

"I've been doing that since day one!" she screamed back in typical Jennifer fashion.

Click.

I could have punched a wall, I was so frustrated dealing with Drew's developing situation and having a demented psychopath of a kid's mother - I began counting to ten in my head.

Calling back wasn't going to change anything. Jennifer was always going to act like Jennifer. The only thing that would change her would be a lobotomy, which I would happily pay for.

Pouring another drink then walking into our bedroom to see Maria in the mirror brushing her hair, she asked me the obvious:

"What's wrong, honey?'

"Apparently I'm acting like a bitch for expressing my concerns about Drew's transition to North Carolina."

She turned towards me, her natural beauty momentarily distracting me from my mental nightmare called Jennifer. Maria spoke, asking...

"Why do you care what she says?"

"I don't," I told her, "but I care about Drew thinking it's ok to act like a little fairy."

"Don't talk like that about him!" she said coming to Drew's defense. I tossed back another shot placing the shot glass on the dresser asking her...

"Hold up, am I wrong for wanting him to act like a normal boy his age?"

"No, you're not," she said, "but he's not normal and neither are you! Look at how you live your life."

"What the hell are you talking about?" I asked.

"The way you make so much money, that's not normal," she pointed out.

"I don't hear you complaining, Maria. What would you have me do work at McDonalds and get shot dead one night over somebody else's burger money by two assholes?" I shouted at her calming down before continuing, "You're comparing apples and oranges!"

Spinning around I picked up my keys heading for the front door saying, "I'll be back, I'm stopping by the studio!"

"Ok, Mr. Normal," she replied. "Have fun with your gay rapper friend!" she laughed.

I paused. looked over my shoulder and flashed her a grin, shaking my head because she was right...

What is normal?

CHAPTER TWENTY-THREE

My responsibilities as Erick Sermon's manager kept me busy on tours across America, Europe and South Korea, filming music videos, attending radio interviews, photo shoots and speaking engagements, not to mention endless hours mixing in the recording studio. My time was more than occupied.

In the midst of all that I was still making plenty of street money, so I treated myself to a platinum colored Mercedes Benz S.500 with 21" chrome rims that I added as a nice touch. The car was fast, classy and fun to drive as heads turned wherever I went and this day was no different.

Pulling out of Erick's driveway, my Nextel chirped showing Jennifer's call number. They say everyone in life has their own personal demons that haunt them in their own private hell - she was mine.

"Hello?" I answered zipping around on this sunny day, a little surprised that she ended her three - month stretch of not calling me since she moved.

"Eddie, I have a problem," she bluntly said. *What a shocker*, I thought, she's only calling when she needs to be rescued. Somehow, because she caught me in a festive mood, I decided to make her work for my attention and so I did my best Jay-Z impression rapping through the phone

"I got 99 problems and you ain't one!" I shouted as I hand drummed the steering wheel, nodding my head to the bass in the background, cracking the window for comfort.

"Can you ever be serious... shit!" she barked. Her attitude wasn't killing my good mood and just to spite her lowering the volume of the Benz radio I asked her playfully...

"What-is-the-e-mer-gen-cey?"

"The kids and I are sitting in the car because we don't have any electricity in the house. I need $600 to get it back on," she said.

The vision of her and the kids huddled in her car with no electricity in the house while I was driving a car worth more than her house tore at my heart strings, not that I had one for her but let's just say she caught me on a good day.

"Yeah, I'll send you a western Union, but why would you wait until they turned the electric off?" I asked knowing deep down and from past experiences asking her a common sense question won't get me a common sense answer, as it never did. But since Drew was born, I spent my life asking her anyway. If she gave any answer that wasn't a deliberate hang up click, then she was having a good day, which happened to be today.

"As soon as I go down and pay the bill it will be turned back on so don't worry about it." And why I jumped before my own common sense kicked in, is beyond me, but just like that, her wish was my command, only because of the children. Of course, if it wasn't for them, she could burn the furniture in the middle of the living room to get light.

"Ok, I'll head to the Western Union now," which I did pulling off the Holbrook exit and in front of a check cashing place with a huge line - an added bonus of my errand for Jennifer. Better give Maria a heads up, so I dialed her number.

"I'm at the check cashing store to send Jennifer a Western Union because their electric got turned off for non-payment. I'm on my way to you as soon as I'm done."

Twenty-five minutes later; money sent, rolling in the Benz, reading off the confirmation number to Jennifer over the phone.

"There's an extra $400 dollars so don't let this happen again," I warned her.

"Believe me," she said. "I didn't want to have to call you at all, but thanks anyway."

"How are the kids," I asked curiously. I still pictured them somehow seeking refuge in the car...

"They're fine," she said, "but we got to go and pay the bill."

"Ok, tell Drew to call me," she hung up normally with me, the first in a long time.

Forget love, I mused to myself. "Money-Cash-cold hard green that's the key to baby momma management."

Maria in all her beauty was standing curbside wearing a black mini-dress, clutching the white Louis Vuitton hand bag I brought her a week earlier, matching her blouse. She looked at me with curious eyes full of questions I already could guess about what - *but I spend my days spoiling the attractive ladies in my life who drive me crazy and I love every minute of it*, I thought, flashing her my million-dollar smile stepping out of my new toy.

"I'm grabbing some cash," I told her skipping steps two at a time. "Wait in the car," I said dashing through the front door. After taking two grand from my hidden wall safe upstairs, I was back face to face with the eyes full of questions whose mouth said what her eyes could not as I jumped back in the driver's seat pulling off with Maria in the passenger seat asking me:

"How much did you send Jennifer?"

"A thousand dollars."

"What!!" There's no way she had an electric bill that high!" she said.

"It was only $600 but I threw her an extra $400 just in case she needs it," I said nonchalantly. After all, I was a wealthy entrepreneur and throwing money at all the women in my life was as common as breathing air, and the only people who noticed or asked for it were the people who didn't have much of it.

Having high amounts of cash around wasn't my main thrill anymore, actually I was bored talking about it, when really it was the lifestyle I enjoyed. Traveling the world, being a key figure in the underground both legitimately and illegitimately. It was my life and I was loving every second of it even when Maria, who now crossed her arms, didn't appreciate me and gave me her "I'm not happy look" even though I spoiled the shit out of her.

Why can't I have one day when all the women in my life are happy? Just one day, I thought taking a short cut through the back streets to get to Red Lobster. Checking my diamond studded Rolex to see if we would still be on time to catch the lunch specials, another thing I loved was a deal!

"Must be nice," Maria sneered with a strange smile I picked up in the reflection of her passenger side window. Her Latin accent always made her sound sexy.

"What?" I asked her smiling.

"To be able to pick up the phone with a sob story and get a thousand dollars in less time than it takes us to get to Red Lobster."

"It's the only time she asked for help since they left," I said and don't know why I'm now finding myself defending Jennifer but that's the way it sounded.

"Believe me, honey, I know bitches like her, this is just the beginning," she warned in her all-knowing woman wisdom.

"Beginning of what?" I asked even though I already knew.

"You'll see," she said looking out the window at the passing world beyond the glass almost whispering, her eyes looking at me in the reflection unsmiling...

"You'll see."

With Drew's 12th birthday coming up, I wanted to surprise him with a visit, and at the same time, see from myself the type of conditions he was living in down in North Carolina.

Jennifer called me two weeks after sending her the Western Union as if to remind me it was that time of the year.

"Drew's birthday is coming up," she announced after a quick hello.

"Yeah, I know that Jennifer."

"He wants a party at the local roller skating rink, and I can't afford it."

"Say no more. How much will it cost?"

"They have different packages. The one for $400 takes care of everything, food, cakes, skate rentals, everything."

"Sounds good, I'll send that today," I told her, adding, "I'm going to come down and surprise him at the party."

After a slight silent pause, she said.

"Uhhh, ok."

"Yeah, I'll fly down that Friday and stay for the weekend. Don't tell him I'm coming. I'll show up at the roller rink."

"He'll like that," she said.

*

I checked into the Radisson Hotel, just three blocks from the roller skating rink. Just as planned around 7:30 Jennifer pulled besides the rented Lincoln Continental I was in with Drew and four girls in her gray Oldsmobile.

Drew was so caught up in his conversation that I went unnoticed.

"Happy Birthday, Drew," I called to him as he began to walk towards the roller rink.

Spinning around at the sound of my voice he yelled, "Daddy!!" running into a warm embrace.

"I wanted to surprise you for your birthday."

"I'm surprised," he said beaming from ear to ear.

Proudly he introduced me to his girlfriends as Jennifer took the lead as we walked inside the lobby of the rink.

Crowded with teenagers wearing baggy pants, and all the latest fashions, huddled in small groups laughing aloud, chasing each other, skating across the lobby, the rink was filled with kids of all ages and a few adults spinning around the loop of the rink, under disco lights and fast tempo hip-hop music.

Walking over to Drew, Jennifer passed him some tickets. I followed right behind him as he walked into the main section to enter the rink when Drew abruptly turned around placing his hand on the center of my chest for me to stop.

"This is my space, Dad, no parents allowed."

"Don't you want me to hang out for your birthday?' I asked half smiling, a little confused.

"This is my time with my friends, Daddy. Pick me up at 10:30pm." Spinning back around, he dashed inside the rink disappearing into a crowd of people his height, wildly excited.

Turning around looking for Jennifer, who was nowhere in sight, told me something wasn't adding up. At 10:30 pm, Drew came outside and jumped in the passenger seat putting on his seat belt.

"How was your night?" I asked.

"Oh, it was fine, I love this place."

"Where are your friends?"

"They have a ride coming to get them, we're good to go dad."

"Ok, are you hungry?" I asked as I pulled away.

"Starving," he said throwing me off a little.

"Didn't you eat in the rink?"

"Nah, they don't have no good food there."

We went to a diner Drew liked and ordered our meals to go. Back at the hotel, I sat on my queen size bed, me eating a turkey burger enjoying the both of us talking. I enjoyed watching him eating his chicken fingers crossed legged on his bed, flipping through the channels of the TV.

"How was your party?" I asked.

"What party, Dad?"

"Didn't you just have a birthday party at the roller skating rink?"

"No, I go there every Friday night to hang out with my friends," he told me matter-of-factly, before turning back his attention towards the television.

My blood began to boil, and I could feel my temperature rising by the second... *that lying bit...*

"Did your mother's boyfriend Anthony move out?"

"No, he still lives with us," he said.

"Well, did he lose his job?" I asked.

"Nope, he still works at the movie theater and gets us in for free all the time."

"So why didn't he help your mother with the electric bill when your lights went off?"

"What are you talking about, Dad? The lights were never off," he said throwing me a look like I was an idiot.

The following morning, I could have confronted Jennifer but I didn't want to risk blowing my visit with Drew.

I kept my mouth shut. In the meantime, I took Drew and Alexis shopping for impulse gifts.

That Saturday night in the hotel room Drew was happy talking about his social on goings with his new friends.

As we finished off the chocolate ice cream from room service, I probed a little bit into his personal life.

"I'm glad you're popular and making new friends son, but you haven't mentioned any friends that are boys," I told him.

It was a weird line with Drew. I knew I didn't want him liking boys rather just having normal boys that were friends. And did want him to do all the boy things that are normal at that age, like playing outside, sports, video games and talking about girls... he flashed me a non-concerned look between spoonful's of ice cream, and told me "The boys don't want to play with me, and I don't want to play with them either."

Placing the ice cream dish on the night table between our beds I asked, "Why don't you want to play with boys?"

"There just too immature and childish; I'm good with my girlfriends."

*

Sunday morning, I drove Drew home, with plans on eating lunch at the house so I could see where he was living. The three-bedroom apartment turned out to be a three-bedroom trailer. It was relatively new on a nice size lot backed up by a thick forest at the end of their backyard.

It was a hot bright day with the country smell of pine and fresh air. The lawn was lush, green, and manicured bushes hid the brick foundation the trailer was sitting on. Maybe the country wasn't as bad as I thought.

"Come on in guys," Jennifer greeted us opening the screen door.

"How you doing, Jennifer?" I asked her thinking I hated how she smoked in front of the kids as I saw the Newport cigarette hanging off her lip.

A new living room set made me think of the money she scammed out of me using Drew's phony birthday party as bait... I clenched my fist, smiling tight-lipped spotting the 42" TV I brought Drew as a show piece for her living room.

"I'm doing fine," Jennifer said.

I bet you are, I thought.

"Drew, show your dad your room."

"Ok, come on dad," he grabbed my hand and pulled me down a short hallway, passing a small bathroom and another little room that I could tell was Alexis'. At the end was a door of cheap and hollow balsa wood leading to Drew's domain.

I'm going to lose it right here, right now, if I walk in and see pink bed comforters, and Wonder Women posters, and God help Jennifer and her punk ass boyfriend if there is a Backstreet Boys poster above the bed... I will burn this whole place to the ground if there is a Back Street...

"C'mon dad," Drew's voice snapped me out of my nightmare and tugged my hand pulling me inside. I actually closed my eyes walked in a few steps opened them and...

Normal blue bedspreads, normal grey rug color, normal video game system, little TV and scanning as fast as I could, I saw no Barbie dolls or pink Power Ranger toys...phew!!... I wiped the imaginary sweat from my head, I was relieved.

"I told mom to take my TV. I'm good with this smaller one because the one you brought took up too much space.

"That was nice of you," I replied.

"I know it's a lot smaller than my room at Grams house but at least I don't have to share it with Alexa."

"Yeah, plus you don't want to be in your room too much, it's good to play outside," I advised.

A knock at the front door caught my attention as I looked to see Pattie walking in with Alexis at her side.

"Hi, Alexis," I greeted.

Her eyes wide and bright, she smiled giving me a big hug and kiss.

Pattie joined us for lunch and as soon as we finished eating, Drew walked me out to the car.

"When are you coming to visit again?" he asked.

"I was going to ask you the same question."

"When school is over, I'll come up for the summer."

"School just started a month ago, maybe I'll fly you up during one of your breaks."

"Ok," he replied with a smile.

"You know we all miss you right?"

"Yeah dad, I miss you guys too."

"Well, come give me a hug so I can go."

Squeezing him tight, planting a long kiss on top of his head, I repeated, "I love you Drew."

"I love you too, Dad, thanks for coming."

*

"Didn't I tell you... Mr. I'm sending an extra $400 just to help out?" Maria poked.

"She won't get me like that again."

"Please, Eddie, you got too good a heart and that's why she always takes advantage of you."

"Believe me, the only money she'll get now is from child support. Drew's clothes, sneakers or anything else I want to get him, I'll buy up here and mail it Fed Ex... without the receipts!"

Maria picked me up from my return flight, leaving the J.F.K. Airport, pulling the new ML Benz truck I brought her onto the Southern State Parkway. She headed east as she continued:

"Jennifer don't know how good she has it. Alexis's father doesn't buy her anything and doesn't pay his child support if I don't take him to court."

"Maybe that's what I need to do."

Turning on the music, relaxing the passenger seat back, I was glad to be back on Long Island.

"No, you don't, and you won't because you're a responsible father and you love Drew. Jennifer knows that and uses it against you."

"It sounds like you're calling me a sucker!" I said cracking the window to get a smell of that Long Island air, still fresh with a hint of exhaust fumes from the traffic.

"You are a sucker, but I love that about you," Maria replied looking at me flashing a wink and a smile.

A few weeks passed without hearing anything from Drew or Jennifer. I was anticipating the next sob story she would run on me to get me to go to the Western Union. When my Nextel flashed Jennifer's number, I inhaled deeply to stay calm allowing it to ring 2 more times, exhaling then answered.

"Hello stranger," I mused.

"How are you doing Eddie?"

"Real good, busy renovating the house. Maria's really looking forward to moving in."

I couldn't resist that little jab to push her buttons.

"That's great to hear, you two are really serious."

"Yeah, she's the one. How's Drew doing?"

"Umm, he's fine, but I have a situation."

"Let me guess, the situation is the reason for this call."

Hold up, cool down I told myself, don't show her your hand. "What can I do to help with your situation, Jennifer?"

"I'm 2 months behind on the rent, and if I don't give the land lord at least $500 today, then me and the kids will be evicted."

"Evicted! Damn, Jennifer, I can't let that happen. Give me about 30 minutes and I'll call you with the Western Union number."

"Thanks, Eddie, I really appreciate it."

"No problem. How's Drew doing?"

"He's fine, still at school," she answered.

"Tell him I said he's old enough to call me, I haven't heard from him."

"Ok, will do."

"I'll speak to you in a little while."

Thirty minutes later, she called back.

"What's up, Jennifer. I was just about to call you, you have a pen and paper for this control number?"

After telling her a 10-digit confirmation number, I told her to repeat it back to me to make sure she had it right. About 20 minutes passed and Jennifer was ringing my phone again.

"Hello?' I answered.

"Eddie, there wasn't a Western union matching that number."

"You sure?"

"Yeah, I'm sure I just came from the drug store."

"Read me off the control number, I have the receipt right here."

She read off the 10-digit code and then I said, "The last number is a 7 not a 3."

"Well, you told me 3 before," she barked.

"I'm sorry, I meant to say 7, but problems solved."

"Ok, bye."

Ten minutes later she called again, but I didn't answer. The control number I gave her was fictitious, I wasn't sending her shit. Three more times she tried calling, before she got the picture, leaving me a nasty message explaining how I'm such a punk ass bitch, ranting and raving about how bad a father I am, and I'll be lucky to ever see Drew again.

Her message had me crying tears of laughter so hard that my stomach hurt. I ended up pulling my Benz over on the side of the road in order to gain my composure. I couldn't wait to get home and play this back to Maria.

"That girl's a lunatic," Maria commented after we listened to the message for a second time while eating dinner.

"I know and she tried to hit me up for $500."

"She would have got it too, if you didn't go down for Drew's birthday," she added.

Pulling a Heineken out of the refrigerator, wrapping the bottle with a white napkin, popping the top off and passing it to me, she asked, "Do you think it was a good idea to mess with her like that?" "Man, fuck her! She brought that on herself."

Taking a sip, I momentarily contemplated the possible ramifications of my practical joke.

"What if she doesn't let you see Drew?"

A concerned expression was clearly on her face.

"Drew's not a baby. He's 12 years old and mature enough to call me on his own, which he hasn't done. But he's old enough to demand to want to see me."

"But you know how crazy his mother is?"

"That ain't nothing new Maria. I'm getting tired of fighting to stay in his life."

"What's that mean?"

"From what I saw in North Carolina, Drew's more comfortable playing with girls instead of boys. How am I supposed to have a son like that?"

"Eddie, you already have a son like that. How you deal with it reflects the type of father you are."

"Technically and biologically yes, that's been proven," I said hitting the pause button to emphasize my point. "But if you or he thinks I'm going to have any type of relationship with him if he decides to be gay, you'll both be wrong."

"You don't decide to be gay, stupid," she shot back.

"So you're telling me he just talks girlish because it's in him? All the sucking his teeth, rolling his neck, what's that? In his D.N.A.? No, he chooses to talk and act like that."

Unpausing my game, looking back at the screen, Maria continued to come to his defense.

"Some of Drew's behaviors were impressed on him by his crazy bitch of a mother, some of them weren't. You have to accept him regardless if he's gay or not."

"Can we not talk about this now? I'm trying to enjoy some down time."

"With playing your dumb game?"

"Yes!"

"Wouldn't you rather spend time playing with me upstairs?"

"Hmmmm, nah I'm good," ducking my head, laughing, avoiding Maria's on coming slap.

Jumping up to leave, Maria reached the doorway, turned and said, "Maybe Drew gets his weird behaviors from you!" She always knows how to push my buttons as she dashed up the stairs to our bedroom with me in hot pursuit.

*

At LaGuardia Airport, waiting to pick up Drew for his summer vacation, I called Jennifer to make sure he made the flight. We hadn't spoken since I pulled my prank.

"Hello?" she answered.

"Jennifer, I'm already at the airport and just wanted to make sure there wasn't any problem with Drew making his flight."

"We were running a little late but he made it."

"Ok, then, I'll have him call you from the car."

I wanted to keep the conversation short and simple. I was about to hang up when I heard...

"Eddie!"

Here we go, I thought. She's probably about to bitch and complain with regards to the Western Union or ask for some money.

"What's up?" I asked.

"Can you keep him," she commanded more than posed as a question.

"He'll be with me most of the time but Drew will be spending time with his grandmother also at her house, it's three weeks," I explained, looking up at the terminal board seeing that Drew's flight had just landed.

"No," she continued, "I mean can you keep Drew for good?"

This shit never ceased to amaze me, last time we spoke it was all "I'm a punk ass bitch, never been a good father, lucky if I ever see him again" and now she was asking me to keep him.

"No problem, Jennifer," I said hanging up the phone without asking any questions or willing to hear her explanation. I didn't have the time for that. Drew would be coming through the gate in a few minutes, and I needed to get things in order. Anytime things get critical, there's only that one number I call...

"Mom!"

"Hey Ed, did you pick up Drew yet?"

"I'll have him in a few minutes. I just spoke to Jennifer and she asked me to keep Drew for good," I anxiously explained

"That's great son, I'll have his room ready."

"Mom, she wants me to keep him permanently."

"I understood the first time, and I'll enjoy the company. Just relax, we're going to be all right."

As always, she said just what I needed to hear.

"Ok, Mom, we'll be there soon."

Still not spotting Drew in the crowd, I made another call to Maria.

"Hey Sweetheart."

"Hey you have Drew yet?"

"No, he should be with me in a minute but I spoke to Jennifer and ..."

After explaining what happened I was hit with a lot of why questions, to which I had no answers. Standing at the gate searching the dwindling crowd for a sight of Drew, I saw him walking towards me, talking it up with the flight attendant escorting him to the gate. After showing my I.D. to confirm who I was, Drew said, "Yeah, this is my dad."

Giving me a big hug and a kiss, I had a big smile as I put my arm around his shoulder and began walking with him towards the baggage claim; in the nine months, Drew had grown quite a bit.

"We've missed you and we're happy you'll be staying with us. Grams is waiting on you right now."

"I can't wait to see Grams, it's been too long," he answered.

"Are you having problems in North Carolina? Because when I was a little older than you, something happened, and I had to go live with my dad." And then I told him about when I was in a similar situation.

I was getting into fights at school and acting out at home at 16 years old thinking I was a grown man. After having a big argument with my mother, I left and went to Jennifer's house who I was dating at the time. Thirty minutes later, Mimi was knocking at the door, I answered.

"What's up, sis?" I asked shocked that she was there.

"Go say good-bye to Jennifer, you're coming with me." It wasn't a request.

"Where?" I asked.

She gave me one of her looks that said "don't ask and not to test her patience", I went and said good-bye to Jennifer, leaving with Mimi who was waiting at the door. As I opened the passenger door of her blue Escort, I noticed two suitcases in the back seat.

"You going somewhere, Mimi?"

She put the car in reverse pulling out of the driveway. Looking me right in my eyes, slamming the car in drive, she answered.

"No, I'm not going anywhere, you are."

"Where am I going?" I asked thinking she was joking.

"You don't want to listen to Mommy, then you can't live there. Dad will pick you up at the airport."

Two hours later I was sitting on my luggage in the Rochester airport for about 45 minutes until I saw my father walk in. With a big smile and arms open out stretched, we embraced with a strong hug and he said, "You must be giving them hell down there." My dad chuckled.

I just shook my head and smiled grabbing my suitcases as we walked towards his van.

"Why you so late?" I asked. "I've been here for almost an hour."

"Eddie, your sister called me and told me that you had to come live with me. I thought you would come in a few days. When I asked when you would be here she said, "he landed at the airport 20 minutes ago."

"Oh," I said as he laughed about the entire situation.

I finished the rest of the 10th grade at East Side High school in Rochester and came back home in the summer.

*

Maybe the reason Drew had to stay was because he's finally allowing his male hormones to take over and needs my manly guidance.

Praying that the reason was due to him acting more like an adolescent boy, he candidly replied, "No, Mom had another baby so there's no more room for me in that house."

"Your mother had another baby?" I asked without hiding the surprise in my voice.

"Yeah, a boy with Anthony," he replied nonchalantly, and then directed his attention to the luggage conveyor belt.

"That's mine, Dad," he said pointing to a large blue suitcase.

"I got it," I said swinging it off the conveyer belt.

Walking towards the parking garage, half listening to Drew since my mind was still racing with angry thoughts about Jennifer, and how hurt Drew must feel at being told there wasn't any room for him at the house.

"Dad!" Drew's voice snapped back my full attention, "this is your car?"

Forgetting that Drew never knew I brought a Benz, I had popped the trunk loading his luggage without noticing how excited he was.

"Yeah, you like the rims?" I asked.

"They're cool, you're definitely the man," he said grinning from ear to ear as he opened the passenger door.

"Well, you're the man next to the man," I replied.

Driving back, I reassured him how happy we all were that he would now be living back in New York. Maybe this is what I need or better yet what Drew needs in order for him to change.

CHAPTER TWENTY-FIVE

Drew didn't have to be the new kid, starting all over, living on Long Island. He was given the choice of living at my house or with my mother, and of course he picked to stay with his Grams, where he already had a room of his own and could keep her company.

Drew's best friend Vinny still lived right next door, his other friend Kevin lived down the block, and they were like the three musketeers playing every day so hope appeared to finally be on my side. We spent a lot of that summer fishing on my new 28-foot Maximum boat, just the two of us mostly, out in the Atlantic Ocean a few miles off the coast of Fire Island.

We caught flounders, red snappers, blue fish, and nice striped bass. Fishing was one of the things my father did with me, but we would always fish from land, enviously watching the real fishermen going out into deep water in their nice boats. Now we were the ones who were looked upon as we slowly made our way through the channel, waving to those on shore as we would head out to sea.

The best part of the trip for Drew was when it was time to head back. He would climb on top of the cabin at the very head of the boat, turn around and yell...

"Go fast, Dad!!"

As the boat would bounce up and down, crashing through the waves, the ocean water soaked Drew. It was quality time we both enjoyed with no distractions from my phone or anyone else.

I noticed that Drew wasn't speaking as girlishly but it would seep out every once in a while. Maria took notice to the shift in his behavior and brought it to my attention.

Having dropped Drew off back at my mother's after he spent a few days at the house with me and Maria, she felt the need to voice her opinion after what she observed.

"Eddie," she said as soon as I came in. "As soon as you left this morning or any time you leave, Drew changes so much."

"Changes how?" I asked closing the front door since she didn't give me a chance to fully enter the house before she started in with me.

"He starts acting like the Drew we all know exists," she replied.

"What does that mean Maria?"

"He acts more lady like," she said with a smirk, knowing it's a topic I'd rather avoid. *I'm going to need a drink*, I thought to myself as I walked into the kitchen for a double shot of Grey Goose.

"I think he's starting to act more normal, and it might take a while but he's playing with boys his age, spending more time around me which I think is a good influence to get him back on track."

"Really?" she said, "because anytime you're around, I notice he's more quiet and careful of how he speaks and acts because he's scared of you."

"Scared of me?' I repeated. "Your exaggerating Maria, Drew knows how much I love him." I proudly stated.

"But does he know you'll still love him if he acts the way he does once you leave, because the second you step out the door, it's like he's breathing a sigh of relief."

"Drew's not scared of me Maria."

"No, he's not scared of you like he's in the presence of physical danger, it's more that he fears the possibility of losing your love. How many times have you told me you'd stop being his father because he's gay?"

"If he turns out to be gay," I cut in, "which hasn't been determined yet." I answered throwing back the shot.

"Drew's not gay, he's just a little feminine from living with his crazy ass mother," I added.

"Well, answer my question," she continued her interrogation.

"I can't answer the question and don't have to answer because my son's not gay!"

"But what if he turns out to be gay, would you still love him?" she asked.

Clearly, Maria had me up against the ropes but I continued to duck and dodge as much as I could.

"I'm not going to do the what if's or would I, should I, could I. If we have to cross that bridge, I'll deal with it then." I told her wishing that my phone would ring so I had an excuse to leave. No such luck.

"Eddie, when you left earlier this morning, I was playing my salsa music while I was cleaning, and Drew came and showed me how he could dance, and let me tell you...he was dancing just like a girl. I told him that's not how boys dance! He just sucked his teeth and continued shaking his hips, hands held high moving like the queen of the night," she explained.

Maria was being serious but teasing me at the same time, while making it clear that it wasn't looking good for the home team. She wasn't done...

"You might not be ready to admit it Eddie but if ever there was a kid that's going to be gay, it's Drew, and you have to love him no matter what, it's important that he knows that."

The voice in my head was screaming, *Nooooooo!* hearing the truth of what she was saying. I didn't want Drew to fear me, if there was anyone he was supposed to feel comfortable and safe with it was me. Hearing that he was attempting to conceal his flamboyancy when in my company, fearing the loss of my love made me feel like shit.

"Drew, knows that I love him," was all I could say.

"But you have to let him know that you'll love him even if he's gay!" Maria reiterated.

"I'm not planting that seed in his mind," I said.

"Sweetheart, that seeds taken root, been cultivated, nurtured and is about to sprout," she replied, leaning over to give me a comforting hug. If it was anyone else, I would be angry or embarrassed, but Maria had a way of rationalizing my responsibilities as a father.

"Can we try to be a little more optimistic?" I suggested.

"Optimistic, yes, delusional no honey, you need to have a serious talk with Drew, and if it turns out that he's not gay - which I doubt- then he knows he's blessed with a father that loves him unconditionally, the way I love you."

"The way you love me huh?" I said standing up from the couch walking to get a refill.

"I'll talk with Drew next week when we go fishing."

The following day traffic was light coming home from the city so I arrived at my mother's at 4:30pm. Since I was early to pick up Drew for dinner plans, I decided to log on to my mother's computer, surfing the web to pass the time until Drew came home.

Out of nowhere, I'm hit with a pop-up showing two grown men shaking their bare asses in my face, asking me to click on to see more. At that moment, the dangers of the internet became real to me.

Quickly clicking off the ass shakers, I began to check which recent web pages that had been accessed. There were a number of X-rated male porn sites, that a part of me wished was a new fetish that my mother picked up.

I had seen enough. Clicking off the computer, I called my mom.

"I was just on your computer, Ma, and these homosexual web pages popped up on your screen. Please tell me you're investigating something for work."

"Calm down, Ed, Drew was exploring those sites, I forgot to mention it to you."

"How could you forget something like that? I'm probably going to have to pay a thousand dollars to get hypnotized so the memory can be blocked from my mind!"

"These things happen at this age, you can't over react," she said.

"Who's overreacting. I've been responding to all of Drew's antic's pretty well as far as I'm concerned, but this shit is getting out of hand, I just can't understand it!" I was pacing back and forth in her little voodoo room as I heard Drew announce himself coming through the door.

"Hey Dad!" he yelled.

"Give me a second, I'm on the phone," I answered. "Mom he just got here, and we're going out to dinner, I'll see you when I drop him off."

"He's just a curious adolescent, son. Don't make a mountain out of a mole hill."

I found myself hitting her with a sarcastic, "Really? I'll see you later Mom," hanging up the phone just as Drew walked in the room, embracing me with a hug.

Hugging him back, looking down at him pretending to be oh so innocent.

"You ready to go get something to eat?" I asked.

"Yeah, can we go to Dave and Busters?"

"If that's what you want," I said as we headed out the front door.

Walking to the car contemplating what to say, how to bring it up, wondering what answers and solutions I have that would be compatible with logic in the mind of a 12-year-old. All was coming up blank. As I sat in the driver's seat, Drew closed the passenger door. I started the car but hesitated before putting it in gear, turning asking.

"Drew, are you gay?"

Looking back at me with utter surprise he quickly shouted back, "No!" with a look in his eyes like a deer caught in the headlights.

"If you are, it's all right, I understand and it will never change how much I love you."

"I'm not gay, Dad, why would you even ask me that."

A long list of reasons raced through my mind: dry humping your uncle in diapers, favorite color was pink along with your favorite Power Ranger, talking like a girl, not wanting to play with boys in North Carolina, not to mention the dance routine that Maria told me about. But I simply said "Well, I was on the computer and some gay websites popped up, I was on the phone with Grams about it, she's not the one who's been on those sites," I explained.

After an awkward three-second silence...

"I was just surfing the web and came across them so I just explored it," he explained.

"Why are you exploring male porno sites and not the girl ones?"

"I went to some of them, Dad, I don't know."

It was clear that he was uncomfortable, shit I was uncomfortable. I just put the car in gear, rubbed his head and drove to the restaurant in silence.

We pulled into the parking space and both stepped out of the car.

"Drew," I called, "come over here."

Eyes locked on mine as he walked around the front of the Benz, I just opened up my arms and embraced him in the longest tightest hug I can remember ever giving him. He needed it just as much as I did because in that hug was an unspoken communication, that explained we were both unfamiliar with the situation as it is, with neither of us having the resolution.

We weren't honestly facing the totality of the circumstances at this time, but the door had been cracked.

The "Pink Elephant" was in the room, but neither of us were prepared to discuss it. I asked him if he was gay and he said no, that's all I wanted to hear. That hug was to reassure him that even if it wasn't what I wanted to hear, we would find a way to make it through together. Until that Pink elephant started stepping on our toes, I was not going to bring it up, hopefully he wouldn't either. We enjoyed our dinner that night, just the two of us, and the pink elephant. The inquiry made us both uncomfortable, but to a degree I could sense Drew felt some relief.

*

My mother was waiting to see how I handled the situation, when I dropped Drew home.

"How was dinner, guys?' she asked as soon as we walked in the door.

"It was good, Grams," Drew replied. "Dad took me to Dave and Busters so I got to play the Dancing game I told you about."

"I'm glad you had such a good time," she said looking towards me as she hugged Drew sending me one of her classic motherly smiles.

"Run upstairs and take a shower, I want to talk to your dad."

"Ok, Grams," Drew said, dashing up the stairs, throwing a last, "and thanks for dinner Dad."

"You had me a little anxious, Ed. You sounded pretty upset when you got off the phone."

"What did you expect ma?"

"Did you guys talk?" she asked pulling out the kitchen chair for me to take a seat.

"Yeah, I asked him if he's gay, he said he isn't, and I told him I would love him no matter what. Then we went to dinner like it never happened."

"Well, that's not a bad start," she replied.

"A bad start to what, Mom. Cause I don't know what a good start is supposed to sound like. I'm in uncharted waters here."

CHAPTER TWENTY-SIX

Searching for a solution where we could find common ground relating to one another, seemed more difficult every time I thought about it, leading me not to think about it and just dealing with situations as they came.

Surprisingly, Drew made it through his last year of middle school without any incidents. I anticipated a call from the principal, explaining that Drew was being bullied or picked on, but it never occurred. Not to say that it never happened, but if it did, Drew kept it to himself and handled it on his own. Who could blame him for not mentioning anything to me even, when I asked, after the way I mishandled the time he was being teased about his girlish voice in elementary school. High school was now on the horizon, but first we had another summer to contend with.

Drew was old enough to stay home alone during the day, since my mother's house was on a safe, close-knit block. When I wasn't away on tours, my days were relatively flexible so I had a routine of stopping by with lunch to check on Drew.

On one visit, I brought two-foot-long subway sandwiches with the works and two large cokes with ice to wash them down. Drew and I sat at the kitchen table enjoying lunch together.

"What plans do you have for today?" I asked after swallowing a bite of my food.

"Probably ride my bike to the school playground with Vinny and Kevin," he answered.

"I'm surprised the two of them aren't over here already."

"They'll be here soon or I'll go to their house, what are you planning?" he asked.

"I'm about to go to the city for a meeting."

"Who you meeting with?'

"Motown Records. We're going to get Erick a new deal, as a matter of fact, let me start to head out in case there's traffic. I don't want to be late."

Wrapping up the second half of my sub to eat on the road, I made my way out the front door.

"Be good and stay out of trouble. Grams will be home around 5:00pm," I said as Drew finished off the rest of his sandwich.

Talking with his mouth full he said, "No worries, Dad, have a good meeting."

Jumping in my Benz for the 45-minute drive into Manhattan, traffic on the Long Island Expressway was light, making for a smooth ride. Reaching for my cell phone to call Erick to make sure he was on time is what made me realize that I left my Nextel on the kitchen table. Ten minutes into the trip, I was taking the next exit heading back to my mother's to retrieve my cell.

Now I was running late, so I pulled up into the driveway, left the car running as I hopped out, and raced to the front door.

Turning the knob, slamming my shoulder into the locked door, I was stunned because even at night my mother doesn't lock the door.

Knocking hard as hell, like the police do right before they break down the door, Drew jerked it open with a shocked expression on his face.

"Why in hell is the door locked? What were you doing?" I demanded to know.

"I wasn't doing nothing, you scared me the way you were banging on the door," Drew answered.

As he was saying this, I noticed that the end of a condom was hanging out of the front side pocket of the tan khaki shorts he was wearing.

"You weren't doing nothing, huh? Then what's up with that?"

Drew was silent.

Walking in the house I did a quick sweep of the first floor to make sure he was home alone.

"What were you doing?" I asked again as I grabbed my phone from the kitchen table.

Drew's face was beat red from embarrassment, his eyes looked up from the floor as he was shaking his head side to side and said.

"I don't know," in a low whisper.

"How don't you know what you're doing with a condom hanging out your pocket?" I asked.

Shrugging his shoulders, looking down at his white Nike sneakers, he finally said, "I was just experimenting with putting a condom on because I was curious to know what it was like," he explained then threw my own words at me, "You said I'm at the age where it's normal to be curious."

I stood staring at him for a moment as he held my stare.

"You're right, I told you that," I admitted, "and I want you to know you can ask me questions about sex with girls," I emphasized.

This caught us both off guard. I was relieved that no other boys were in the house and that the computer was off because I don't know how I would have reacted. A quick glance at my watch showed I was running late. Drew was relieved knowing I had to get to my meeting.

Walking towards the door I said, "All right, Drew, we'll talk about this later."

"Ok, Dad," he answered, closing the door as I jogged to my car.

Once I was back on the expressway, a hysterical laughter took over, picturing all the thoughts that Drew must have had running through his mind when he heard me banging on the front door like a mad man.

The image of him whipping the condom off, stuffing it so carelessly in his pocket, while pulling up his shorts, had me crying tears.

I never mentioned the condom incident to anyone at that time because I didn't want to embarrass Drew. This situation was a lot different from the computer pop-ups, where I wanted Drew to feel embarrassed by whatever was attracting him to that life style.

CHAPTER TWENTY-SEVEN

In my mother's neighborhood, a few of the properties on the block had in ground pools where most of the kids would go swimming. Drew, Vinny and Kevin liked to use the above ground portable pool my mother brought from one of her infamous garage sale adventures.

It stood about 4 feet high and the boys used it as their own personal wrestling ring. Watching from the kitchen window on a muggy afternoon, all 3 of them were having one of their free for all battle royals, grappling with one another while exchanging head locks, clothes lines, and body slams on their own personal water arena. Watching the innocents of being youthful doing things that boys his age usually do kept the sanity all fathers in my situation would cling to.

When Drew started watching WWF, I familiarized myself with the current wrestlers so we could have a good common ground for discussion.

"You still think Triple 'H' can beat the Undertaker?" I asked as we sat on my mother's couch watching one of the matches.

"Any day, Dad. Once he does the 'Pedigree' it's over for whoever's in the ring," Drew stated with an exciting confidence.

"Steve Austin beat him, that's why he's the champ," I shot back shoving him challengingly. With a smirk on his face, shaking his head, Drew told me his expertise.

"That was a fluke! He'll get him in the re-match at the Wrestle Mania that's coming up."

"I watched the first Wrestle Mania when I was your age. Mr. T and Hulk Hogan paired up to be the tag-team champions."

"They're old men now, Dad, that's ancient history," he said.

"They could still give the wrestlers of today a run for their money!"

"What?" Drew answered in defense. "Big Show, Da Rock, Mankind, X-Pac and even Chyna would put those senior citizens on their backs 1, 2, 3."

Drew would throw me completely off at moments like this, going from one end of the spectrum to the other. How can "Queer Eye for the Straight Guy" be his favorite TV show, but then be a WWF fan at the same time? Unless he's watching the wrestling for a completely different reason, but who knows what's going on in the young mind of his.

Since Drew was approaching his 13th birthday, I surprised him with a limo to take the 2 of us along with Vinny and Kevin to Madison Square Garden to watch WWF live. Playing the cool dad, I rode up front in the passenger seat with the driver, giving Drew and his friends the freedom of being somewhat unsupervised.

Fooling with all the buttons and switches, blasting the radio, they were making faces and sticking up their middle fingers at people that passed by to see if the tint on the windows really worked, again just enjoying life.

At Madison Square Garden, I took the boys around to the side entrance, meeting some of the wrestlers before the match.

Once inside I brought every snack they had, plus merchandise like tee shirts, and WWF brochures, anything Drew and his friends wanted. They were VIP tonight. The arena's energy was electrified as we made our way to our seats.

We weren't situated ring side, but we were still relatively close to the action. The boys were cheering, booing, having a great time watching the different matches. During a short intermission Drew looked up and asked:

"Can we sneak up a little closer to the ring for the next match, Dad?"

"As long as you don't get in trouble and stay where I can see you."

"Cool, come on guys," he shouted to Vinny and Kevin.

"Drew, if you can't see me, that means I can't see you, so make sure we lock eyes," I reiterated.

"Ok, Dad," he answered as he pushed his way passed me out into the aisle.

The three of them maneuvered their way through groups of people, dodging the ushers and blending in with the crowd standing just a few feet from the ring. Drew looked back and waved, I waved nodding my head, giving the okay sign.

The lights dimmed until darkness fell onto the crowd, thousands of people eager for a show, music blasting just as fireworks exploded from the center of the ring. When the smoke cleared, beautiful, big-breasted women in G-string swimsuits stood in the center of the stage, making the crowd go wild as they seductively squared off with one another for a good old fashion cat fight! Every single guy in the packed audience cheered! They even had me making my way up closer to get a better look, while at the same time keeping my eye on the boys.

They were pointing, laughing, fired up with excitement. Drew playing right along with his friends whistling, shrieking and howling at the erotic exhibition taking place in the ring. As Drew's father, knowing what I knew, I just took full joy in the moment, recognizing it for the illusion that it was.

After the event was over, we went to dinner and the boys again enjoyed the same antics on the ride home. We dropped Vinny and Kevin at their houses and I walked Drew into my mother's house.

"Did you have a good time?"

"Yeah, Dad, this was like the best night of my life, thanks a lot," he answered with a smile.

"Thank you for being such a wonderful son."

"It comes pretty naturally."

Giving him a big hug and wishing him a Happy 13th birthday one last time, I kissed the top of his head and left to go home.

CHAPTER TWENTY-EIGHT

The entertainment business opens the door to knowing people in diverse forms of entertainment. I still wasn't ready to give up all hope and throw in the towel with conceding to Drew being gay. Willing to go to any extent available, I decided it was time I take the gloves off, pull out the big guns and do what any loving father faced with my situation I'm sure would be willing to do, and I knew exactly who to go see to help remedy this situation.

Diamond had long black hair, green eyes, puffy lips, a small frame with tea cup breast. She was a 21-year-old exotic stripper who did some escorting on the side. She'd been dancing at Illusions since she was 18 and was always in high demand.

I preferred the thick breasted, ass clapping females, but when one of Diamond's co-workers let her know I managed Erick Sermon, she came and introduced herself because she was also a singer.

Promising me the world if I would manage her, I told her when the time was right I would consider it.

She was busy giving a lap dance to a sweaty overweight drunk guy in a cheap suit when I walked in the club at 2:30 am after leaving a studio session in Manhattan. I ordered a double shot of Grey Goose at the bar and was quickly approached by China, who's half black and Asian with a body like a Coca Cola bottle.

"Tell Diamond that Eddie's here, and when she's free, I would like to go to the Champagne room," placing a twenty in her hand to deliver the message.

"I'm not pretty enough for the Champagne room, Papi?" China asked over the sounds of Kanye West and Jay-Z's collaboration. Leaning over brushing back her black long hair to speak right into her ear I said:

"You are sweetheart, you definitely are," I told her, rubbing my hand down her thigh, slightly caressing her fat ass, "but I promised Diamond I would come see her, you understand right?"

"I guess, but could you make me that same promise?"

Turning around wearing nothing but a G-string she slowly walked off towards Diamond, looking over her shoulder sending me a seductively promising stare.

Diamond's eye's popped wide when China told her my message while pointing in my direction. She's probably thinking I was here to talk with her about her music career, but other more important business was on my mind. Whatever Diamond said to the guy she was giving the dance to made him clench his thick cigar like eyebrows together shaking his head no, revealing his disappointment at what he heard. The appearance on his face brightened up as China took over, putting a smile back on the happy customer.

Walking as fast as she possibly could in those red nine-inch high heeled stripper shoes, Diamond politely declined all offers from other patrons, making her way to where I waited at the bar.

"Hi, honey! Long time no see!" grabbing my face and kissing my cheek.

"Nice to see you pretty lady," I replied.

"The Champagne room is a minimum of $250 but I'll make it a night you'll never forget," she said with a smile.

"Listen, I just need to go somewhere so we can talk without being interrupted."

"All you want to do is talk?" she asked surprised.

"Yeah, I have a business proposal, a special job that I need you to do."

"Eddie, I never thought you were one of those kinky types, but I heard you're a freak," she joked giving me a nudge.

"That I am sweetheart, but I'm not too kinky, this really doesn't have to do with me." I told her.

"How about I save you $250, take me to get something to eat, I'm at the end of my shift."

At the Hilltop Diner a few blocks away from the club, I watched as Diamond started in on her second deluxe cheeseburger. Between bites she explained back to me what I proposed.

"So let me get this right," pausing to take a long sip of her diet 7-Up. "You want me to play the role of your son's babysitter, and then seduce him into having sex with me."

"Yes, that's exactly what I want you to do."

"How old is your son?" she asked.

"He's 13."

"Let me guess, you're scared he might be gay?"

"How did you know that?"

"You're not the first paranoid father I've met."

"Tell me you've cured other boys of this before."

"I don't think of it as a cure. He either is or he isn't or maybe he's into both, you never know."

"That doesn't sound to promising," I said feeling a little defeated.

"Listen, one time this quiet, sweet, little 12-year-old, who at first look I thought for sure he was gay, ended up making love to me like a grown ass man. Another time a 15-year-old boy, who was on the football team with the body of a NFL linebacker ended up straightening my hair, painting my nails and giving me a few fashion tips," she said taking another bite of her second burger.

"Well, let's hope and pray it's not a beautician's lady's night."

"Since he's a younger version of you, I hope so too, but it's going to cost $1,000."

"A thousand bucks!!" I shot back at an attempt to negotiate.

"Yeah, your son is a minor and if anyone knows the theory about more risk more reward... It's you" she countered.

"You're right," I said finishing off my black coffee as I signaled the waitress for our bill.

I agreed to call Diamond during the week to finalize the details of my master plan to get Drew to see what the hell he's missing and hopefully save him from himself.

Reservations for dinner were made on Friday at 7:30 pm at Gasho's, a Japanese restaurant in Brentwood. It was Maria's favorite restaurant so I planned to have her meet me there, and surprise her with spending the night on the town. After dinner we would head to Manhattan and go to club Copacabana, where they play salsa music on the main floor and hip-hop in the room downstairs. That would keep us out of the house until at least 4 am. Alexa was at her grandmother's in Rhode Island, leaving Drew plenty of time to be transformed from a sissy acting boy, into a man!

I called Drew on Thursday to make sure he would be ready when I came to pick him up the following day.

"Hey Daddy!" he answered.

"What's up little man?" I asked.

"Nothing much just chilling."

"Well, tomorrow I'm going to pick you up to spend the weekend. Maria and I are going out Friday night, but I have a sitter staying with you until we get back because early Saturday I got something for us to do," I explained.

"Did you say sitter, like a babysitter?" he questioned, then added, "cause I'm too old for that, Dad."

"Yeah, I know, but I don't want to have to rush our night if we're having a really good time. Just to have no worries, my friend's daughter will keep you company."

"Whatever, if you say so," he answered.

"I'll pick you up around 5:30 pm."

"Ok, Dad."

Everything was going according to plan. Diamond would be at the Ronkonkoma train station at 6:30 pm for me to pick her up and bring her to the house where Drew would be, and from there I'll go meet Maria at Gasho's, beginning my night of celebration because this had to work. That Friday heading over to pick up Drew from my mother's house, thinking to myself *why couldn't I have a father as cool and as down to earth as me?* When I was 13, something like this was a fantasy straight off the pages of the Penthouse magazines I used to read, having me praying to God this type of experience would happen to me. Now I'm driving on my way to make it happen for my 13-year-old son, and I felt damn proud about it, saying out loud, "I am a great dad!" with a smile.

Pulling onto my mother's street, grinning from ear to ear, satisfied that I was taking the right steps of any loving father, my grin quickly faded when I saw my mother's white I-30 Infinity I brought her parked in the driveway, home early from work. This wasn't expected, I was just going to leave her a letter or call letting her know Drew was with me like I always did. Anyway it shouldn't be a problem. "Hello!" I said announcing myself as I stepped in the front door.

"Hey Ed," my mother answered from in the kitchen.

Walking over I gave her a big hug and kiss instinctively sensing something odd but couldn't really tell what it was.

"Where's Drew?" I asked.

"He's out riding bikes with his friends," she answered.

"But I told him I was picking him up for the weekend."

"Yes, he mentioned that to me last night."

This isn't good, I thought to myself and asked, "So why isn't he here?"

"Because I told him you'll pick him up tomorrow morning since you're going out, and he's too young to be at your house alone all night with some stranger."

Oh, shit, I thought, the way she emphasized stranger with that glaring stare of hers, reminded me why my friends nicked named her the "inspector" when I was a teenager.

"She's not a stranger, Mom, it's one of my friend's daughters who needed to make some extra money for school."

"Drew is going to be staying here tonight. I don't have any plans and I can drop him off in the morning or you can pick him up. This way he can play with his friends like a boy his age should be doing, and you could save your money." Explicitly stressing the "save your money" phrase sent a cold chill up my spine, warning me that my plans have been compromised. Having enough street sense to leave well enough alone, I made nothing of it as if it was no big deal. But then she asked...

"Eddie, did you hire that girl to have sex with Drew?"

"What! No, Ma, why would you think something like that?"

"Because I know you better than you think I do."

"So you think I'm the type of father that would hire an escort to have sex with my son?"

"Yes, unfortunately I do," she answered.

"Well, I've never even thought of anything like that, but since YOU brought the idea up, maybe it's something we should explore before it gets too late."

Why did I say that?

I was bombarded with a twenty-minute lecture of the many morally ill consequences that could result from those type of actions, how that wouldn't change a thing if Drew actually was gay, and how I would be contributing to confusing him even more.

Silently I listened thinking, how much more confused can he be? At his age what better way was there to un-confuse his mind? Just three years earlier Drew was playing with Barbie dolls. I wanted to let him have some fun, with a real girl and see if there's a change in his behavior. My mother wasn't open to this idea at all, she was disappointed that I would even consider going that far, but from my perspective, to not do this would be neglecting my responsibilities as a father.

After a drawn out reprimand and a few promises from me to never attempt to do something like that with Drew, I left, but not before giving her a kiss good-bye.

It was another defeated effort to save Drew, but I wondered if he even wanted to be saved.

CHAPTER TWENTY-NINE

I had recently gotten arrested in Washington Heights carrying $28,000 in a Louis Vuitton duffle bag on my way to put a down payment on a future transaction. Bailing out the following day, I was informed by my lawyer Paul that the money was being seized and we would have to go to Civil court to get it back.

The last thing I wanted was any government agency asking about my finances, like the letter I had just received from the North Carolina child support services. Throughout the duration of Drew living in New York, I continued to make my child support payments because I hadn't taken the time to go down to Family Court to get the order rescinded. Plus, I just didn't want to deal with Jennifer's drama. But this was too much, so I went to the Central Islip Family Courthouse with all the documentation that proved Drew was in my custody for the past 2 years. It wasn't as quick and easy as I expected.

Jennifer contested the order, and why wouldn't she, being that she was getting free money from child support. Jennifer was definitely going to make this an issue with her vindictive attitude that always seemed to take a simple situation, -making sense to any sane person coping with logic and reason- appear as if I had some type of attack specifically against her.

This was exactly the kind of drama I didn't want to deal with. The Judge set the date for the end of the following month. Since I had so much documentation of Drew living in New York, she suspended temporarily my child support payments.

Prior to any of this, any time Drew wanted to visit his mother, there was never a problem. I would pay for his round trip flight, whenever he asked. A week after I went to family court, Drew surprised me with a call.

"Hey Daddy!" he said when I answered my Nextel as I was in the recording studio with Erick.

"What's up Drew is everything ok?" I asked.

"Yeah, why?" he asked.

"Because you don't call me much, I always call you so I thought something was wrong."

"Well, times are changing, things never stay the same dad."

"Oh yeah, so what's up?"

"I just wanted to go visit my mother," he stated.

"Sure you can visit after we settle this Court situation."

"What's the situation?"

"No big deal, I'll pick you up when I'm done in the studio in about an hour and we'll talk then."

"Ok," he said hanging up the phone.

A little over an hour later, at the sound of my beeping horn, Drew came running out the front door with a huge smile on his face.

"I already ate with Grams, Dad," he said closing the passenger door.

"Do you have some room for Carvel ice cream?"

"Even if I didn't, I'd make room for that honey," he girlishly answered.

"Honey?" I said as my eye brows slanted downward in an angry expression.

"Umm, I meant Dad." He quickly cleared up, "I thought you were Grams."

Letting his slip of the tongue slide, I pulled off towards the ice cream shop and began our much needed conversation.

"Drew," I said as he stared back at me with his full attention.

"I understand that you mother and her family always painted me as 'Mr. Bad Guy' in your eyes," I began.

"No, not really," instinctively defending them.

"Cut it out, Drew, let's keep it real. You're old enough that we can have this talk," I said.

"Yeah ok, maybe sometimes they did," he finally admitted.

"And I understand that even if you didn't agree with what they said about me, there was nothing you could do because you love your mother."

He just looked up at me nodding his head, I continued, "You've been living with me for these past couple of years, and I need you to understand where I'm coming from,"

Again nodding his head in agreement, as I pulled into the Carvel parking lot.

"Let's get our ice cream and finish this conversation while we eat in the car."

"Okay," he answered.

We each ordered a banana split with butter pecan ice cream, hot caramel, with nuts, Reese's pieces and colored sprinkles on top. Walking out with a big stack of white napkins and 2 spoons, we got back into the Mercedes Benz. Taking a few scoops of my dessert, I thought about where I wanted to go with this conversation. It wasn't my intent to throw blame or use this as an opportunity for revenge to really hate on Jennifer so I just asked him.

"How many different girlfriends have you known me to have, besides your mother?"

"Rosa and Maria," he answered.

I thought he would have remembered Robin but it was such a short time, it didn't matter.

"And how many different boyfriends has your mother had?"

With a mouthful of butter pecan, shaking his head left to right he answered, "Too many to count."

"Obviously, I know how to get along with people, anytime we're out you've never known anyone who's had a problem with me besides your mother and her family."

"They have a problem with everyone," he said tapping right into my line of thought.

"Exactly my point, Drew. It's something you need to take a look at and think about, when you consider how I'm blamed for everything that's wrong in everyone's lives by them."

Again he nodded his head in agreement, eating his butter pecan, enjoying every bite as I continued.

"The reason I'll send you to visit after the Court date is that I suspect your Mom might try to say you haven't been living up here all this time."

Still nodding his head, he continued eating away.

"Even while you've been here, I've continued to pay the child support and that's what this court hearing is about. You understand?"

"Yeah, I hear you," he answered.

"I shouldn't have to continue to pay your mother since you're living with me."

Drew looked at me as if what I had been saying finally got through and said, "Yeah, you shouldn't have to pay anything since I'm here with you."

"Right!" I said adding, "I'm not asking for support from your mother either, I want you to know that."

"Well, that's cool" he said.

"So after the Court hearing, I'll order the tickets and you can go for a visit."

"Sounds good to me, Dad."

"Ok then, let's finish this ice cream before it melts, then I'll take you back home."

*

Arriving at the Family Courthouse in Central Islip with my mother, the court clerk informed me that Jennifer was opposing my request to no longer pay her support and was scheduled to appear via telephone link. Sitting in the gallery wearing a dark blue Jones New York suit, white shirt with a black tie, I whispered, "You see what I'm talking about, Mom. Jennifer is going to make this some drawn out drama issue."

"Don't worry, Ed," she whispered back. "Just remain calm and polite with the Judge no matter what Jennifer says" giving my back her all too familiar motherly rub.

"What's Jennifer going to say? Yes, Drew's been in my custody but that doesn't mean I should stop helping to support her?"

"Who knows what's on that girl's mind, just remain..."

"Wright vs. Romero," the court bailiff yelled into the room.

Walking right beside me like a high paid lawyer, my mother looked at me nodding her head with a smile giving me the go ahead to present my case.

I finished explaining the situation on how it came to be that I've had custody of Drew along with my mother and thanking the Court for allowing me to present my case. The black female Judge, in her early fifties, looking down at me through the top of her glasses, began to address me, "Mr. Wright, before, and while this hearing has commenced, my clerk has tried to contact Mrs. Romero to no avail. Therefore, I'm in full agreement with everything you've presented to the Court and terminate the order of child support. You have a right to receive child support from Mrs. Romero and she has a parental obligation to pay just like you have."

"I know she would but I'm not the one that gets extorted, I do the extorting. Drew's allowing himself to be manipulated by that crazy bitch!" I said raising my voice.

"Daddy, watch your language, no bad words!" Alexa shouted, pointing her finger at me.

"Sorry angel, you're right," I said shooting her a smile as she slowly turned back to watch TV.

"Drew has me pissed. All he ever does is whatever makes his mother happy."

"Well, it's his mother, he's young and you can't hold it against him," Maria said.

"But I'm his father and he's quick to say fuck me!"

"Daddy!!" Alexa shouted giving me another evil stare.

"I'm sorry sweetheart; I'm just a little upset."

Standing up, pulling out Maria's chair so I could kneel down in front of her, I lifted up the red blouse covering her stomach, placing my ear against her belly, listening for the sound of my daughter's heart, saying a silent prayer to myself to not make the same mistakes with her that I made with Drew.

CHAPTER THIRTY

The Bureau of Alcohol, Tobacco, Firearms and Explosives arrested my street lieutenant. I received a call from my lawyer Paul after he investigated what lead to the charges.

"The news isn't good, Eddie."

"What type of threat am I facing, Paul?"

"Why don't we just talk in my office?"

"Ok 5:00 pm good for you?" I asked.

"Yeah, I'll clear my appointments."

Paul wanting me to come in to talk told me things really weren't good. This couldn't have happened at a worse time. The baby was due in two months, Erick and I were negotiating a new deal with Koch records, and I was renovating my mother's house. Sitting in traffic on my way from the city, the onset of a headache began throbbing on the side of my temples. Turning down the music I hoped the silence would ease the pain for a few minutes so I could get my thoughts together. Just then, the cell phone rang showing Maria's number.

"What's up fat girl?" I answered.

"Just here all bloated ready for your baby to get out of my stomach."

"A few more months and she'll be here."

"Easy for you to say," she said. "Anyway, I'm calling because your man called and said to turn on the bat phone."

"Ok," I said reaching in the glove compartment, grabbing the pre-paid phone, pressing the power button.

"What time will you be home?" Maria asked.

"I'm stopping by the studio, and I'll head that way," I explained without bringing up my meeting with the lawyer.

"Good because we have Lamaze class at 7:30 pm in case you forgot."

"I didn't," I lied, "and wouldn't miss it for the world."

"You better not," she said hanging up the phone.

While approaching exit 56 on the Long Island Expressway, the prepaid phone that only one person used showed a New York State prison number.

"Yo!" I answered.

"What the fuck is going on?" my friend asked.

"Why?"

"I had an unexpected visit this morning."

"From who?"

"The alphabet boys, offering me a ticket home."

"That's what they do," I replied.

"Then you already know," he stated.

"Yeah, what's understood don't need to be spoken."

"Ok, then you be safe."

"You too," I replied hanging up the phone.

We both knew it's never safe to speak openly, keeping it short and simple. Enough was said for me to get the complete picture with what was going on. At the studio my mind was racing, watching the clock until it was time to leave for my appointment.

I pulled up to Paul's office, parking my Benz right next to his champagne colored Porsche that I'm sure I paid for. Walking into the lobby, I was greeted by Janice, Paul's secretary, who you could tell was a real looker back in her day. Now in her late 40s, she was still attractive, especially with her big welcoming smile. After pushing back her chair, she stood up and walked around the front desk to greet me with a strong hug.

"Mr. Wright! Great to see you."

"Nice to see you, too."

"Paul's expecting you, come right in," she said as we made our way to his corner office. Meeting me at the door, Paul invited me in telling Janice to hold his calls.

This was Paul's new office revealing the opulence of his successful law firm. It smelled expensive from the fine quality of the leather chairs. Behind his huge mahogany desk was an all-black, leather-bound, legal library of books with gold lettering stamped on their spines. These were just for show because all the legal information he needed was on his Apple computer that was sitting on the corner of his desk. The huge window revealed the sun setting with some light still streaming through. Pulling out the burgundy leather chair, Paul sat down loosening his black Gucci tie, letting out a deep sigh.

"You look all stressed, what's up?" I asked.

"Things seem to have taken a turn for the worse since we last spoke," he replied.

"Paul, it's only been a few hours, how bad could it have gotten?"

"Bad," he answered. "Since your guy hasn't cooperated yet, they went to visit your friend upstate and offered him a deal."

"I know already, he called. No need to worry though, he's solid."

"Did you talk on a secure line?" he asked in a state of panic, eyes bulging wide.

"Of course, Paul. Calm down."

"Eddie, this isn't the state where I could do magic, this is the United States Government, the big boys."

Taking a deep breath, leaning back with both hands locked behind his head, he continued.

"My source told me my name's even coming up, so I'm not going to be able to represent you."

"Represent me? I'm not even charged!"

"You're not charged yet," he corrected. "But you're the target of their investigation and these people don't play by any rules."

"What do you suggest?"

"Leave the country," he quickly stated without a second thought.

"I got too much going on with the baby so that isn't happening," I answered.

I could tell he wasn't happy with my response, shaking his head as he said,

"You have a choice. They could visit you somewhere in South America or in prison."

"Hold up. Damn, Paul, you're convicting me without being charged. We've been in tight spots before."

"Not like this," he said.

With both elbows resting on my knees, I placed my hands on the side of my head, rubbing the throbbing that once again began in my temples.

"What lawyer am I supposed to use?"

"Pulling out a card, he passed it across his desk.

"His name is John; I'll update him on the situation."

*

For the next 2 months I didn't have time to really worry about how Drew's life was going in North Carolina because I was busy making my legal preparations for my fight against the Feds.

It took me a few meetings with my new lawyer John before he gained my confidence, which in turn meant handing over $100,000 for his services, then another small fortune to a private investigator to find out just how strong a case the Feds had against me. They're not the only ones who do their homework. I needed to know every single detail.

I had to be on my toes as this wasn't the time to slip up. While brainstorming I got an idea. Since knowing the government would set their sights on Maria, the closest person to me and try to get her to flip somehow if they could, there was one way I could prevent that from happening.

"I thought we were going to have a big wedding, Eddie, you promised me," she wined all the way to city hall.

"We will," I confirmed rubbing her hand continuing, "Think about it like this... do we want our daughter looking at our marriage certificate later in life and seeing we tied the knot after she was born? She might think she was unplanned or worse an accident and we can't have her thinking..."

"This just seems so spur of the moment," she cut in, "what happened to all your talk about a pre-nup?"

"I realized, beautiful, that we're never getting a divorce, so let's not jinx it with a pre-nup," I said squeezing her thigh twice in a playful way.

She punched my shoulder. "I'll kill you first anyway before we get a divorce," she threatened through a smile. That smile faded though when we pulled in front of city hall.

We went to the justice of the peace.

Stood at the window.

Paid the fee.

I smiled.

She half smiled.

We signed.

Kissed.

Hugged.

Then left.

I dropped a few hundred on a romantic dinner which was all I could do before dropping off my new, slightly aggravated bride back home while I took off to meet with the P.I., Richard.

We shook hands and I looked him over. Salt and pepper hair, mid 60s, typical retired cop look. We met at T.G.I.F. and I nursed a Heineken while Richard used both hands to dive into a platter of ribs dripping with BBQ sauce.

"Eddie," he said between bites, "I've seen these types of investigations before with the feds; they don't play by the rules. It's hardly what it seems."

"It seems like someone's using me to save themselves."

"Well, that's nothing new," he answered sucking the sauce off the tips of his fingers one at a time and using his cloth napkin to wipe his mouth before adding: "This isn't really about drugs, you know there's a bigger investigation by the organized crime task force, looking into a crooked cop and a string of robberies."

A light went on in my memory, but I kept it to myself.

"They have a bum named Joe in protective custody down in Miami," he said.

"Did he get locked up?" I asked.

"No, he's in the witness protection program but I used some of my contacts and got this address on his current whereabouts," he said sliding a folded piece of paper across the table.

Tiny beads of sweat began popping of my face, and I suddenly felt flushed under the collar. It was like a sauna in the room... I waived over the waitress and ordered a shot of Grey Goose. To Richard, this was everyday 9-5 business as usual, but to me the hour glass full of sand was turned over and I felt the first hint of pressure.

"Give me your un-cut conclusion Richard, from your gut, what do you think?" I asked.

He took a gulp of his orange soda, wiped his mouth with the napkin, dropped it on his plate and leaned in a little and said in a low voice "It's clear that you're connected to a lot of people in powerful places Eddie. You have a lot of valuable information that can help them solve a lot of unsolved cases which you know how this goes, it's a two-way street... you help them out... they might help...

"I'm not cooperating, Richard, end of story. So let's cut the bullshit. What's my chances at trial?" I asked.

He leaned back not satisfied with my convict code stance, so he simply said, "Look, Eddie, as it stands now, good, better than most, but that can change at any time. You shouldn't totally not consider helping the-

"Well," I cut him off, interrupting on purpose, sliding a few twenties into the leather bill folder. "I'll call you if anything else comes up, but keep me posted if anything with our friend in Florida changes."

"Ok, Mr. Wright, be careful and stay safe."

I had no plans on staying safe, it was time to do some investigating of my own.

CHAPTER THIRTY-ONE

Maria's water broke.

Uh-oh.

We dropped off Alexa at her aunt's apartment in the Bronx, and Maria's water broke all over the Benz's passenger seat.

Not cool.

Don't panic.

Stay calm.

Pray there are no serious traffic jams today on the Long Island expressway.

"Are you going to be able to make it to the hospital in Stony Brook?" I asked.

"Yeah, Eddie, I'll be fine. Stop asking!!" she roared.

Maria wanted to take the hour drive in the opposite direction to drop Alexa in the Bronx even though her contractions started earlier today a plan I completely disagreed with.

"Maria, honey, are you sure you're thinking clear. Your idea doesn't sound so-

"Eddie, you're driving me crazy!" she slightly shouted. "Please go to the Bronx so we can drop off Alexa. I have enough to deal with right now, stop asking me stupid questions!"

"Stupid questions," I mumbled under my breath.

"What did you say?" Maria demanded, giving me the crazy *I'm having a baby today. Don't fuck with me look.*

"Nothing Honey," I answered coolly dipping and swerving in and out of traffic.

I saw myself pulling over on the side of the highway, my head caught between Maria's baby spreading thighs, delivering my daughter in the back seat of the Benz with nothing more than a sweatshirt to receive the baby in and a Poland Spring bottle, to clean her off with.

Fuck that...

Flicking my headlights, driving with the hazards flashing, I called ahead to the hospital to let them know we were in route.

My mind pulled together thinking,

Don't crash.

No wrong turns.

No missed exits.

Thirty minutes later, I was wheeling Maria in and hugging my mother in the lobby.

"I told you we would make it and we did, so stop whining."

"Who's whining?" I asked smiling.

"You were," she said, suddenly distracted between deep breaths and closing her eyes trying to relax.

"Try to relax sweetheart, you know I love you."

"No shit, Eddie, did you figure that out all by yourself?" she said then mumbled a swear word in Spanish while closing her eyes again rubbing her belly.

I just looked at my mother saying, "She's a little moody, Mom."

My mother just gave me a big smile as she rubbed my back and now gave Maria and me both comfort as we piled into the elevator and ascended up to the maternity ward.

Nia Marie Wright was born at 8:30 am the following morning, on November 5, 2004.

Her dark brown eyes calmed me as I held her in my arms. Language fails to describe the flood of rising emotions caught in my throat.

"You did a good job, Dad," my mother said wrapping her arms around me, giving all her attention to the newest member of the family, who's temporary nickname was "Bundle of Joy."

"Pass her over to her mother," she whispered.

Maria receiving our daughter jokingly said, "She looks just like you Eddie, except she has hair!"

"Yeah..." I said mesmerized looking at a breathing little angel. I reached for her again.

"Easy, Eddie, can I hold our daughter for at least five minutes?" she asked.

"You've been up all night," I told her. "I know you're tired, get some rest, let me hold the baby."

Reluctantly, she gently passed Nia over to me. We were all smiles watching our little miracle, our new addition, and my new major responsibility. The nurse stepped in and did what they do, and we passed Nia over to her so he could check her vitals and make sure all the little baby functions were in order.

Once Maria passed out, I stepped out and called Drew.

"Helloooooooo," he answered in his most girlish voice.

"What's going on, son?"

"Oh hi, Daddy," I heard his voice sound a little stronger now that he knew it was me.

"We had the baby this morning. You're a big brother!" I told him as enthusiastically as I could.

"Well, that's nice, but I'm already a big brother, Dad," he corrected me.

"I know, I know, son, but you're a big brother again. Your little sister's name is Nia and she's beautiful!"

"I'm sure she is," he said sounding bored. Then he hit me off guard, "You haven't called in a while, did you forget about me?"

"No, not at all, Drew, but you know this invention called the phone works both ways," I said.

"I just don't want to bother you," he replied.

"Drew, knock it off, you're never a bother here,"

Changing the subject, I said, "Say hello to Grams." I made my way over to Maria, caressing her face with fingers and gentle kisses.

"I'm going home to take a shower, nap and to get things ready. I'll be back in a few hours sweetheart." I told her in an almost whisper.

"Okay," Maria replied still in dreamland, turning her head back into the pillow.

"Ok," I kissed her head goodbye, took the phone, and ended things as best as I could with Drew's roller coaster attitude, which was normal. I knew that. I headed to the elevator with my mother, whose back pats as we eased down the hallway, gave me the confidence to put one foot in front of the other.

CHAPTER THIRTY-TWO

No one comes to my house unannounced.

Walking into the study from my bedroom, peeking out of the window where I had a clear view of the front door, I saw two uniformed Suffolk County police officers, knocking, and peeking towards the windows.

I wasn't answering.

Bending down, duck walking back into my bedroom, I retrieved my cell phone, and called my new lawyer John.

"What's up, Eddie?" he asked.

"There are two uniformed cops at my door," I whispered.

"Uniformed cops don't serve warrants," he said as I crept back into the study for another look, spying them ever so carefully.

"If they had a warrant, I doubt they would be knocking," I told him still in a hushed tone.

"It might not be a warrant to enter that house; it has-

"Hold up, John, they're leaving so it can't be that important," I said breathing a sigh of relief.

Still duck walking barefoot into the living room, I watched the police pull out of the driveway and drive down the street.

"Like I was saying Eddie, uniformed cops don't..."

"Oh shit! John, they just stopped at an unmarked car. Hold on."

Scanning the rest of my street, I noticed another 4 unmarked cars, 2 people in each watching my house.

"This isn't good," I mumbled.

"What?" John asked.

"Hold on."

The car that the uniformed police officers were talking with, all of a sudden took off with a screech of the tires, heading right for my house with the other 4 cars following right behind.

"John, I'll call you back!"

Dashing to the stairs leading to the basement, both feet taking flight, I plummeted down to my man cave floor, cutting a quick left into the laundry room, leaping over the Kenwood washer/dryer that blocked the tight crawl space with just enough wiggle room to squeeze my entire body into, so I was under the stairs. The piece of plywood that covered the hole fit back neatly as I caught my breath and listened to the sounds outside.

Boom...

Boom...

Boom...

I listened to them pounding on the door.

"We know you're in there! Open up!" a voice demanded while I stayed quiet, hearing numerous footsteps surrounding the side of the house where a second door, lead right to the basement.

"Look, that's today's newspaper on the kitchen table, he's definitely been here," another male voice spoke, whose face must have been pressed against the kitchen window.

"Come out now so no one gets hurt!" The voice at the front door shouted.

They were going to have to kick in the door and find me, I thought, but then I realized that they must not have a warrant to enter the house, without knowing for sure if I was there. The blue light from my cell phone illuminated my entombed hide out as I dialed the lawyer.

"John," I whispered, even though I was sure they couldn't hear me from outside.

"Are you all right, Eddie?"

"For now, the house is surrounded."

"They must have a warrant for you."

"You think?" I chuckled nervously.

"What are you going to do?"

"My daughter was born today, I have to spend some time with her," I said undeterred.

"Eddie, maybe you should just turn yourself in," he advised.

Jerking my head back, looking at the phone, I wanted to fire him for saying that and had to hold back from screaming.

"John, my movie isn't going to end like this, not today. I'll call you later."

"I'm here," he said weakly.

The longer I stayed hidden under the stairs, the more my confidence built up in figuring a way out of this predicament.

After an hour under the stairs, and not hearing any movement around the outside of the house, I withered my way back upstairs, keeping low to the floor, creeping up to the front window, careful not to move the venetian blinds.

Surveying the street, I spotted 2 unmarked cars parked 3 houses away, nose ends facing my house.

"God!" I called out loud. "I know I maxed out my credit card with you, but I need an extension to spend time with Nia."

The silence right after made me listen for a response. Nia's angelic face flashed into my mind. I would have more time with her somehow, some way. As soon as nightfall set in around 6:00 pm, I crawled out the window into the backyard, jumped the fence and ran a few blocks over where a friend was waiting to take me to the hospital. Once we left the neighborhood, riding on the highway, I called John.

"Eddie, you had me waiting with this phone on me all day," he answered.

"It took me a while to get away from the house but I made it," I answered.

"What's your plan?'

"Not sure yet, just wanted to let you know I made it out."

"Ok, keep me updated."

"Will do," I said hanging up the phone.

Walking into the hospital ward, I felt a knot in my stomach knowing that I had to come clean with Maria. Entering her room, finding her breast-feeding Nia was a picture-perfect moment locked in my memory to this day.

"You took yourself a long nap, Eddie. What you don't miss your daughter?" she said with a smile on her face as I slid myself onto her hospital bed.

"You wouldn't believe how much I missed the both of you, and what I had to go through to get here."

Telling her the truth was the hardest thing I ever put her through but it had to be done. Unloading the day's events, and what I had been dealing with for the past few months, Maria began crying scared for herself, our daughters and me. I calmed her as much as I could for the next three days as I hid out at the hospital.

When the time came for Maria and Nia to be discharged, I began to stay in an apartment I had in the city.

For the next two months, I worked on stacking as much money as I could and at the same time going back to Long Island, renting hotel rooms to spend time with Nia. I was getting my time with her but I always felt the count down until my capture in the back of my thoughts, loud sometimes, like a gong banging the seconds away.

When my street lieutenant's girlfriend called me to ask to speak with someone that owed him some money, I agreed to meet her in the city, next to the sneaker store where he worked. It was December 10, 2004 and she had the feds waiting on me when I showed up.

"Your Honor, Mr. Wright's charges carry a minimum of 10 years and a maximum of life. He's the head of an elaborate criminal enterprise. For these reasons our office strongly requests that bail be denied," said the Latino, United States prosecuting attorney.

Standing up dressed in a navy blue designer suit, taking a sip from the glass of water, then placing it back on the table, John addressed the court.

"Your Honor, Mr. Wright has lived in Suffolk County for 33 years. He has strong family ties and is willing to put up two properties valued at $750,000 to secure his appearance. He's not charged with anything violent and denies any knowledge or involvement in the prosecutor's claims. Therefore, I'm requesting the court grant bail so Mr. Wright can adequately prepare for trial."

"Bail is denied!" the Judge announced.

Fuck! I silently cursed.

Maria and my mother stood in the galley of the court crying tears, seeing me wearing an orange jumpsuit, hands cuffed, being lead to the holding cage to be transferred back to M.D.C. Brooklyn where I had been for the past month. It was time to make the call I'd put off in the hopes I would make bail.

"Daddy, why's that recording saying you're a federal inmate?"

Drew asked after pressing the number five to accept my call.

"I'm in a pretty bad predicament and it appears that I'm going to be here at least until I go to trial."

"Oh my God, Dad!"

"It's all right, no need for you to worry. I just wanted to call and let you know myself," I said leaning my face against my forearm, posted up on one of the four phones they had in the unit. It was hard not to let tears flow for his sake.

"But what happened?"

"Drew, I can't talk about it on the phone. It's a misunderstanding with my taxes."

I hated lying to him, and it was a juggling act to keep my emotions in check.

"Oh," he said a little calmer.

"You know how much I love you?"

"Yeah, I know."

"Ok, well I'll call when I can," I said.

"All right, Dad. Take care."

Hanging up the phone was tough. Walking back to my cell to lay down, hearing Drew's voice was pulling me towards a state of manic depression. I closed my eyes and wanted to disappear.

The following week I was transferred to Nassau County Jail for pre-trial, it was closer to the house and more convenient for my family to visit.

*

Drew had plans to come to Long Island along with the rest of his family the following summer after my arrest. So I called Jennifer to arrange to have him come visit.

"How you holding up?" she asked after accepting my call.

"I'm fine, just wanted to set up Drew coming to see me when you're in New York."

"That's no problem but I need to bring him," she answered.

"He can come with my mother or Maria."

"Eddie it's a traumatic experience. I need to be there for him."

"Really, Jennifer, he's 14. It's not that serious."

Her seriousness for Drew's emotional safety was a little late, I thought, raising an eyebrow.

"Well, I'll have to think about it," she answered.

I politely got off the phone without smashing the receiver repeatedly into the wall. I pulled myself together noticing all eyes were on me and then called Mimi.

"What's up, lil' bro?" she answered.

"Mimi, you'll be coming home when Drew is visiting right?"

"Yeah, that's the plan so all the grandkids could be together, why?"

"Look, call Jennifer and arrange it so you bring him to visit. She wanted to bring him, and you know it would start something with Maria." I explained as if I didn't have enough problems without the baby mama drama.

"You know how she is."

"I'll take care of it." She assured me.

"Ok, then I'll see you soon."

*

Walking into the visiting room, Drew was cuddling Nia in his arms with Alexa following behind holding Mimi's hand. The whole scene was picture perfect and put a smile on my face.

"Hey Dad," Drew greeted while passing Nia to Mimi, he reached over the waist high barrier to embrace me with a hug. Drew's presence brightened up the room and made my day.

"Look at you all tall and grown. I've missed you," I said rubbing his head both of us laughing.

"I've missed you, too," he answered all smiles.

Greeting the rest of the family and after settling into the visit, I wanted a couple of minutes with Drew alone.

"Mimi, take the girls to the vending machines for me."

She got the hint "Let's go, girls," she said taking a slow stroll to get some snacks.

"Drew," I said as he stared at me smiling his famous smile, "I wanted to talk to you alone to apologize for being here."

"You don't have to do that, Dad," he replied.

"Yes, I do. Especially to you"

"Why?"

"Because the girls are too young to know what's really going on, and you're at an age where you really need me to be there, and I'm not."

"Dad, it's all right, I'm fine. Just work on coming home."

"I'm working on it, son."

The hour-long visit flew by, and before I knew it, the C.O. came over to tell me my time was up. After hugging and kissing the girl's good-bye, I grabbed Drew in a strong hold and I said, "I really am sorry, Drew."

"Don't be, Dad, you're the best."

It was hard to let him go. I did physically, but not in my heart.

Watching them leave the visiting hall, all smiles waving to me, a lump formed in my throat as I fought to hold back tears. I had fucked up the most important thing in my life, and like all fathers standing in my situation, I knew it, even though all my actions were to make them better off. Drew was approaching difficult teenage years, when it's critical to have a father figure in his life, and I was back to being telephone dad, writing letters expressing how I would be there for him. It wasn't the same as being there physically.

*

When Jennifer left a message with my mother a few months later asking me to call, I knew it wasn't good.

"What's going on, Jennifer?"

"What?... It's your son!" she barked.

"Calm down, Jennifer, is he all right?"

"No, he's not."

"Calm down," I said again. "Spit it out. What's the problem?"

"He's being disrespectful and not listening."

"He's a teenager, it's not-

"Fuck that, Eddie, he needs to go live in New York."

Here we go again, I thought to myself. Instead I said, "Jennifer, that's not happening."

"Why not? He's your son!" she screamed.

"First of all, I'm in jail and we're dealing with a lot now also. Second, I told Drew the last time he left that if he didn't come back he would have to live with that choice."

"Eddie, I raised him, you should take him now."

"I'm... in... prison," I slowly stated. "Maria and my daughters are living with my mother now; these are hard times for everyone."

Click!

She didn't understand as usual, she was abrasive and combative. As disappointing as it was to hear that Drew was acting out, there was that part of me that was happy to hear he was giving his mother hell.

"Karma is a bitch!"

The Universe is finally responding with some justice for all the bullshit Jennifer put me through, even if Drew had to be the conduit of the stress, she was going through dealing with him.

However, it turned out to be a double-edged sword when I began to find out just how out of control Drew was.

CHAPTER THIRTY-THREE

In 2008 Facebook was sweeping the world. Hearing about it before I got locked up, it just reminded me of the group chat lines my friends and I used to call in our adolescent years. I wasn't too computer savvy, only using the one we had to book trips with Maria. The impact from the pop-up images on my mother's computer was probably why I limited my internet activity.

A week after telling Jennifer that Drew couldn't move back to New York, Maria broke the news to me about Drew's behavior on my daily call home.

"I spoke with Mimi last night," Maria said after a quick hello and telling me that all was well with the girls.

"Good. How's California?"

"Fine, but it's Drew she called about."

"Let me guess... Jennifer wants to send him out there?"

"I doubt your sister would take him after what he posted on Facebook, and even if she did, Shawn wouldn't have him around the boys."

"Hold on, you lost me... posted what on Facebook?" I asked wondering what the hell she was talking about.

"Of Drew dancing," she said.

"Ok, what's so wrong with that?"

"He's not dancing a little girlish, like with the salsa music. This is a pornographic stripper dance and he has over 5,000 hits already."

"Let's not get over excited, it's just dancing," I said trying to remain calm.

"It's more than that," she replied.

"What's more?" I asked.

"Older men are trying to hook up with Drew. There's a thirty-five-year-old guy calling himself X-mas in July sending pictures of himself, bare chest wearing Santa pants hanging extra low inviting Drew to see more."

My heart rate accelerated, knuckles turning white from clutching the phone, forcing myself to listen.

"Mimi has access to his Facebook account."

"Uh Huh," is all I could manage.

"She e-mailed Mr. X-mas about contacting a minor and said she was contacting the authorities."

"Yeah."

"Then Mimi called Drew telling him to take his performance off the computer because he's dancing like he wants someone to stick something up his ass!"

"Maria!" I shouted.

"What... It's your son", she snapped.

"I don't need to hear shit like that."

"Well, that's what she told him, don't get mad at me," she shot back.

Don't kill the messenger. Don't kill the messenger. Take a deep breath, I told myself.

"I'm not mad, I just got to process all this. I'll call you later tonight."

"Ok, honey," she said.

Shaking my head, walking back to the seclusion of my cell, I thought about a program I recently saw on MSNBC called "To Catch a Predator." It depicted how vulnerable underage children are with internet access by setting up a decoy house where a young teenage child is supposedly home alone, but it's really a young looking cop or volunteer working with law enforcement.

Child molesters make my skin boil and Drew's safety, not knowing what he was doing, was killing me.

On the show, there was a continuous stream of men from all walks of life being arrested. Married men expecting to meet young boys or girls, straight men and gay men, doctors, lawyers even a Rabbi was caught after sending naked pictures of himself to someone he thought was a 14-year-old boy.

Now Drew was on the internet looking to attract this type of attention, not knowing the full consequences of his actions. This was one of those moments I was glad to be in jail, because my gangster mentality would have orchestrated my own catch a predator decoy house, with Mr. X-mas at the top of my list. And the horror I would inflict on him, would get a million hits from Facebook. He would scream in cyber space, and he would be an example for the rest of the child predators.

I never mentioned Drew being an internet sensation with him because I knew he would perceive it as me attacking him and not accepting who he is.

"How's school going?" I asked in our next conversation.

"Fine, no problems."

"You listening to your mom and getting along?"

"Why should you care, y'all don't get along," he barked back sounding like Jennifer.

"I care because I'm your dad and even if we don't get along, she's still you mother."

"Please, that bitch don't care about no one but herself."

"Whoa! Who you talking to like that?" I shot back. "Don't call your mother a bitch, show some respect."

"Respect is given where respect is deserved, I call it like I see it," He said with no fear at all of any repercussions on my behalf, probably because he knew I couldn't get out of prison to deal with him.

"Well, show me some respect," I said.

"Why should I? You're in prison."

"It doesn't justify how you talk to me, Drew."

"I don't need justification."

"Oh yeah, you think you're grown like that?" I asked shocked that he was talking to me like that.

"Yes."

"I'm going to get off this phone before I say something I regret later," I told him.

"Bye!"

Click.

Nothing was getting better.

Nothing.

Waking up with a splitting headache on the following Saturday morning, with the effects of the jail house wine combined with 200 milligrams of Seroquel pills taken the night before, the last thing I wanted to hear was my name called by the C.O. for an unexpected visit.

Taking a quick shower, brushing my teeth, dressing in the orange jump suit, rushing into a pair of white Nike sneakers, finding a sample of Gucci cologne in a G.Q. magazine, ripping it out and rubbing it over my clothes so I at least smelled good while I felt like shit.

Walking into the visiting room with the three long, waist high wooden tables, a short plastic barrier separating us at chest level once we were seated, my mother stood up from her seat on the opposite side with a big smile, wearing a white halter top sweater, blue jeans and brown penny loafers.

Wrapping her arms around me, I returned the embrace, placing a long kiss on top of her head, hoping that the cologne camouflaged the scent of alcohol that was seeping through my pores.

"This is a nice surprise, Mom," I said.

"I was up early and just wanted to come and talk."

"Something going on?"

"Not at the house, everything is fine but I'm concerned with Drew."

"What's wrong?"

"I'm just worried with him living with Jennifer."

I sat back telling her, "Ma, Drew made his choice when he left to live with her and-"

"He was only trying to please his mother so..."

"But right now he's out of control and the last thing you need at the house," I tried to convince her.

"That's because Jennifer's probably not making sure he's taking his medications," she answered, hitting a sore wound from a battle I lost with Jennifer in the past, one in which my mother sided with her.

It stemmed from when Drew was 8 years old and some quack doctor told Jennifer he suffered from Attention Deficit Disorder (A.D.D.) and prescribed him Ritalin against my better judgment.

"Hold up, Jennifer," I protested on the phone from in prison during my time in Virginia. "I've read some bad things about the effects of that drug being given to kids at such a young age."

"He needs something to help him calm down, Eddie. You're not here, you don't see how out of control he is," Jennifer argued back.

"He needs to go outside and play, burn off all that energy instead of watching so much TV," I said.

"It's not that simple," she replied.

"It's not as simple as some pill either. If you're telling him he needs drugs to control himself, what's going to happen when he's older?"

"Eddie," she raised her voice, "You're not hearing me, he needs it, even your mother agrees with me," she said.

It was the first and only time my mother sided with Jennifer against me so there was nothing I could do or say, and I hated everything about it.

Reaching over the clear Plexiglas barrier, grabbing both my mother's hands, staring at the distressed look in her eyes, I said, "Mom, Drew's been told he needs drugs most his life, now he's out of control using alcohol and who knows what other drugs and..."

"That's why he needs my help," she pleaded.

"We have too much going on now, adding Drew to the equation isn't going to happen."

"But I feel like I'm abandoning him," she pleaded with watering eyes. I couldn't turn away from feeling the pangs in my own heart.

"Don't start crying, Mom, you have to let Jennifer handle him."

"She can't handle herself, much less him."

"And you think you can?" I had to ask.

"Better than her."

"No ma!" I said shaking my head. "Drew's staying in North Carolina!"

The finality in my tone was clear so after a momentary silence and a few deep breaths she switched the topic.

"Have you spoken with your lawyer?" she asked.

"Yeah, nothing new just preparing for trial."

"I'll be glad when this misunderstanding is over."

"Me too, but we have to be prepared for the possibility of me doing a little time."

"We'll make it through as long as we stay strong."

I could see the toll this was having on her, and I hated myself for it. After over twenty years of sobriety, my mother left my first court hearing and went straight to the liquor store, gained 20 pounds within two months, and she was taking medication in order for her to sleep at night. All these problems added to my own sleepless nights.

"Let's get through this situation, and once I resolve this, I'll see about moving him back, Mom," I said, ending the visit with giving her the hope she needed to hear, that I needed to hear as well.

CHAPTER THIRTY-FOUR

"You sent Drew where?"

"Job Corps," Jennifer explained, "where he can learn a trade, finish high school and learn some respect."

"Did he want to go?" I asked. "Because that shit sounds like some junior prison type shit."

"He didn't want to go at first but he's learning to like it. I didn't give him a choice, he's out of control."

Struggling to keep my voice calm, I asked, "What's his address so I can write him?"

Once I had Drew's information, I hung up the phone and walked into my cell, writing Drew explaining the difficulties his Grandmother was having trying to cope with my situation and apologizing for not being there to help him with some of the challenges he's facing as a young adult. Writing made it easier to convey that I loved him even if he was acting out.

It took sending five different letters until I got a response from him. Drew opened his letter, thanking me for continuously writing him and apologized for taking so long to write back but he's just been so busy at Job Corps with kids that were in similar situations as him. Without explaining what those similarities are, he kept his letter short. He included a phone number, telling me the best time to call him was around 5:50 pm.

"And what did she have to say?"

"Drew's with her, living in Florida."

"Florida?"

"Yep."

"Is he in school?" I asked.

"That's what she said as if everything is fine and dandy."

"Why did he leave Job Corps?"

"I don't know, Ed, she was very guarded with answering any questions, and I didn't talk with Drew."

"Well, at least we know where he is and he'll fill us in once we talk to him."

Even in the midst of facing the rest of my life in prison, my legal worries were put on the back burner. It wasn't that I didn't care; it's that I cared less about what was going to happen to me and more about what Drew was going through, which was still a mystery to me. However, with Drew's grandmother on the case, I was confident she would come up with a few more pieces of this missing puzzle. All I was able to do was hope for the best.

When my mother gave me Drew's new cell phone number with a message to call as soon as I could -after a month of not hearing a word from him-, I suspected whatever has been going on, finally reached a boiling point to where he felt it was best to get me involved.

Slowly dialing Drew's number, I punched the buttons softly with the tip of my finger as a variety of different scenarios raced through my mind.

Is he going to answer crying, on the brink of killing himself and wanting me to hear his last moments of what being such a bad father caused him to do? Bad thoughts of that conversation showed pictures in my mind.

Or is he about to ask for my blessing so he can elope with his Cuban lover expecting me to welcome him with open arms into the family. A mental image of me physically choking the life out of his Latin lover made my chest constrict just as the phone began to ring, sweating beads were popping on my forehead.

"Drew, what's going on?" I asked as soon as he accepted my call.

"Going through it," he answered with a righteous anger.

"You stopped communicating, left Job Corps and moved to Florida. What's up?"

"I left Job Corps because my mother missed me," he boldly stated.

"Ok, you stopped communicating with me because...?"

"No reason, I'm just busy with my life."

"You sound upset?"

"I am upset, Dad. I just finished fighting with my mother's boyfriend Anthony."

"About what?"

"He hit my mother, and I'm not having that shit. When I defended her, he pulled a gun on me, he's all strung-out on crack."

"Hold up what? When did this happen?"

"Earlier today. Now my mother's kicking me out of the house!"

"Your mother wants YOU out?"

"Yeah!"

"Give me few minutes, I'll call you back."

"Ok, Dad."

Something didn't sound right, this wasn't anything close to my panicked imagination. But Drew's story, protecting his mother from the heavy handed, gun totting crack head, causing her to kick him out the house, forced me to call Jennifer as fast as I could.

"Hello?" she answered surprised that I had her number.

"Jennifer, what's going on with Drew?"

"Your son had a smart mouth, he's disrespectful, and doesn't listen to anyone!" she said on the verge of screaming.

"He told me he was protecting you from your boyfriend whose smoking crack and pulled a gun on him."

"What?"

"You heard me; who's lying you or Drew?"

Click.

"This fucking bitch!" I said out loud furious! While calling Drew back, ignoring the dirty looks from the other guys waiting to use the phone, I shot an *I don't give a fuck* look back and kept dialing the number.

"Hello," he answered.

"Drew, I just spoke to your mother who told me a completely different story."

"Dad, that's Mom calling me on my other line, call me back in 30 minutes."

Click.

This little mother fucker I said to myself.

I called back every 30 minutes until it was time to lock in, but he never answered. The following morning Drew finally picked up.

"Everything's fine dad, we worked it all out," he said right after I said hello.

"And what about her boyfriend?"

"It's cool, it's all good," he answered without giving me any further explanation.

It's very fucking far from all good, I thought but kept it to myself.

"What you told me didn't sound cool."

"Don't worry about it. I gots to go Dad."

"Okay," feeling the brush off, "I'm just checking to see if you're all right."

"I'm fine, we're good," he said.

"Then I'll talk to you soon," I said hanging up not satisfied with how this call ended.

Whatever type of manipulative game this was, if it was an attempt to get Drew to move back to New York it didn't work. Expecting me to say "Pack your stuff and come to New York!" wasn't happening Circumstances had drastically changed. Maria and the girls moved from the house in Ronkonkoma to live with my mother, who was having a difficult enough time coping with my situation.

Since I didn't come to Drew's rescue, all communication was severed for the next year. Mimi continued to keep tabs on him with calls and through Facebook so I was updated on the happenings in his life. During this period Drew graduated high school, an achievement I was extremely proud of knowing he faced immeasurable challenges throughout his young years.

It was a much needed welcomed highlight at a low point in my life. I was confronted with huge challenges of my own during this time, since pleading guilty the day before trial and facing a mandatory minimum of 25 years and was something on my mind 24/7.

"What's wrong, Mom?" I asked hearing the sniffles when she answered the phone.

"Jennifer said she's signing Drew up in the military, where he'll be sent to Iraq!"

"The military?"

"Yes, where he'll be killed!!" she broke down crying.

"Calm down, Mom, you're overreacting."

"I have a right to overreact, it's my grandson's life!!"

"Drew's not going into the service."

"He already signed the papers and just needs to bring his social security card down and it's final!" convincing herself the more she spoke it out loud.

"Listen... to... me..." emphasizing each word. "Jennifer is pushing your emotional buttons, trying to scare you into having Drew move back to New York."

"You don't know that, Ed!" she yelled.

"I do know that, Ma," I yelled politely back. "The military has the don't ask don't tell policy, with Drew you don't have to ask and he can't help but to tell," I said trying to calm her down. Continuing I said, "With all the medications he's been on, they're not going to put a gun in his hands."

"At times of war, this government will make the exception!!" What I thought was my clear logical reasoning wasn't working.

"Trust me, Mom, Drew is not going to Iraq!" I couldn't even picture Drew doing the macho solider scene never mind firing a gun.

"Well, Jennifer gave me Drew's new number for you to call to say good-bye. Why would she do that?"

"Good, give me the number. I'll call you back Mom."

Throughout the years, I've grown accustomed to dealing with Jennifer's manipulative ways, now Drew was showing another sign of following suit. I wasn't having that.

"Hello!" he answered on the second ring.

"Hey stranger, long time since I've heard from you. Did you forget about me?"

"No, Dad, I've just been busy living my life," he answered.

"So what you doing with your life now?"

"I've been to the army recruiter and all I have to do is take the physical, sign the papers and it's all done," he stated.

"That's a great idea, son! I wish I would have joined the military at your age. I probably wouldn't be in here."

"Uh-huh," he replied.

"It's definitely a good move so make sure you send me the address when you're in boot camp."

"Uh-huh," he said smelling the booby trap.

"Is you mother around?" I asked.

"Yeah."

"Let me talk to her."

After a few seconds, Jennifer picked up the phone.

"Hello?"

"Hey Jennifer, how you doing?" I asked sounding extra friendly.

"Fine."

"Yo! Great move with Drew going in the service, it will do him good," I said with nothing but a supportive tone.

"Yeah," she muttered.

"Of course!" I continued. "But before discussing things with my mother, run it by me because she's dealing with too much right now."

"I just told her Drew's plans," she replied.

"Cool, it's a great choice, but my mother's getting old, and I worry her enough as it is. She can't take worrying about Drew getting killed in Iraq," I explained.

"Well, it's possible!" she shot back.

"Yeah, but statistics show it's a slim chance. So if it concerns Drew, get a message to me and I'll call you. Make sure you tell us when Drew leaves for boot camp," I added.

"Ok."

Drew never contemplated joining the military and also didn't consider telling me the truth about what was going on. I wasn't happy with having to play this manipulative game with them, and Drew playing his part the way he did, let me know that our relationship was far from where I wanted it to be.

CHAPTER THIRTY-FIVE

On December 12, 2007, I was sentenced to 45 years and transferred to Lewisburg Federal Penitentiary, an old red brick maximum security prison built in 1933 nicked named "The Big House." Working out, staying busy in the law library determined to fight and win my case on appeal became my everyday routine, the "convict" routine. Two long months passed since hearing from Drew. My mother was in contact with him but he never seemed to answer my calls after declaring my unyielding support of him joining the military.

I received a short letter telling me to call yet another new cell phone number.

"Helloooo," he answered.

"Drew! You're a hard guy to catch up with," I replied.

"Well, a lots been going on, and I'm staying busy."

"How are things with your mother?"

"There cool but I moved out."

"Yeah?"

"Uh-huh, I got an apartment with some friends in Orlando, and I'm working at the McDonald's at Disney World."

Well, of course! I thought to myself smiling, but said, "You're living on your own, taking care of yourself, sounds like you're stepping up with your responsibilities."

"You know it! I'm doing me," he said in his girlish tone.

"You drinking or messing with any drugs?"

"No, Dad, not me, I'm too smart for that," he replied triggering my bullshit meter but I wasn't going to push the issue.

"Hearing from you a little more often will help me out a lot, I'm going through it a little," I admitted.

"I got you, I got you, it's just," he paused before admitting, "I'm busy."

"I was the same way at your age, but at least keep me with your current cell number and answer my calls."

"Ok, will do."

"I love you son."

"Love you, too."

Checking on me wasn't on the top of his list of things he needed to do. Concerned with Drew being only 18 and living with some friends, didn't really sit right with me, but the position I put myself in left me helpless and there was nothing I could do about it.

It was my first time admitting to him that dealing with this hardship was affecting me and it wasn't easy for me to admit it that. I needed some more of his support, but the following week his cell phone was off.

Another two months passed until I finally called Jennifer to ask what was going on.

"Hey Jennifer, how are you doing?"

"I'm good. What's up?"

"Haven't been able to reach Drew, his number is disconnected and my mother hasn't heard from him either which is unusual," I explained.

"I don't know where Drew is and to tell you the truth, I'm fed up with his constant drug use, drinking and disrespect!" her voice raising the more she spoke.

"Drug use and drinking? This is the first I've heard of any of that?"

"That's because you stay in prison!" She barked getting her little dig in on me, then continuing, "Drew's been physically abusive towards me, and he brings all his different boyfriends into my house. I have three young kids to worry about, I'm done with your son!"

"Listen I can hear you're upset but he's still young."

"He's out of control! He got himself kicked out of Job Corps for his drug use and barely graduated High school!"

"But he did graduate," I said.

"You're just hearing about what I've been dealing with for years. When and if I hear something, I'll let your mother know."

"Ok, Jennifer, I'd appreciate that."

Hanging up the phone, then fixing myself a cup of coffee to take to my cell and think, I wondered how different life may have been had I never let Drew go back to North Carolina for that visit. He's at that age, attempting to figure out life and who he is. Now knowing about his drug abuse, I prayed he didn't get lost in the ways of the streets, but somewhere deep in my instincts I knew he already was.

Was he dead? A junkie sticking needles in his arms passed out in a crack house? For over a year Drew went missing and I lost my mind with worrying about him. But when I heard that he landed in a drug rehab center, it actually brought a sigh of relief into my life after all the disturbing thoughts and images that were keeping me awake countless nights.

"At least he's taking the steps to get himself clean," my mother said, sitting in the visiting room of U.S.P. Canaan, the new Penitentiary I was recently transferred to. It was nice seeing her again as she always had a way of putting things into a positive perspective for me.

"How long has he been there?" I asked leaning forward a bit.

"A few weeks," she said adding, "he sounds good and sober."

We both paused a moment taking in this morsel of good news. I sat back asking;

"What type of drugs was he on? What has he been doing for the past year?"

Are you sure you can handle the truth? my mind whispered.

"He was selling and using coke," she said, "living in the streets, having a lot of sexual-

"Mom!! I don't want to hear about his sexual exploits!"

"Well you asked, and he was so...

"Ma! I don't want to know." I reinforced looking her in the eye. She pressed her lips together tight probably holding back more news that would give me nightmares about Drew. "As long as he's still alive then I'm good," I said.

"Yes, we have to be grateful for that," she answered.

Rehab is just a temporary solution to a bigger problem. Drew had a lot of emotional issues that he needed to come to terms with if he wanted to heal himself completely. I personally knew addicts that would get so out of control, - that, even though I was their dealer- I would actually drive them to the rehab center and make sure they would check in.

Dysfunctional addicts can't pay their debt. I wasn't under the illusion that since Drew entered into a drug clinic all his problems would be solved. From my experience, all my customers would party even harder after they came out of rehab. Time would tell if Drew was taking his condition seriously or not, unfortunately statistics and what I've witnessed... probably not.

I couldn't ignore the fact that the way I lived my life, had a deep impact on the choices and decisions Drew was making, and I was sure he was blaming me for the circumstances that he was dealing with. Regardless of how much he was blaming me, he has to understand that it was his life that needed attention.

A month later, Drew was back living with his mother. From what I knew, which was just the tip of the iceberg I'm sure, two months into rehab probably wasn't enough time. Once I knew he was home I called.

"Welcome home, son!" I greeted.

"Hey Dad! It's so good to hear your voice," he replied.

"Damn, man, it's good to hear yours. Drew, you have to keep in touch with me, I can only do so much from in here and I miss-

"Yes, yes I know."

"I was worried to death."

"No need, I'm fine," he said.

"Fine... then how come... I mean... how was your time in rehab?"

"It was hell! But I'm good. Ready to hit the clubs and make up for the time I missed."

That's the opposite of what I wanted to hear.

"Just take it easy and be careful with the choices you're making," I advised.

"I hear you, old man," he said and I could picture him smiling through his words.

"Old man, huh," I repeated with a little chuckle.

"Yeah. When you coming home?" he asked.

"I'm working on it," which was always my response.

"I don't know how you do it. Two months in rehab was torture, you've been there for over five years!"

"I take it one day at a time," throwing some A.A. concepts at him.

"Fuck that! You need to do what you got to do to be free!" he stated.

"It's not that easy, but like I said, I'm working on it."

"All right, Dad, it was nice talking to you."

"It was. Drew stay in contact with me!" I pleaded.

"I will," he said.

"I don't give a fuck how messed up shit may seem; it won't change my love for you." I wanted him to know this.

"Ok, Dad, I got to go, love you," he said rushing me off the phone.

"I love..."

Click.

"...you too, son," I whispered into an empty phone that I held for an extra few seconds before placing it gently back in its cradle, worried about my little boy on the other end who's lost in an adult world.

CHAPTER THIRTY-SIX

"Your son's gay!! How could you even admit that?"

"Because it's the truth," I answered, speaking to my new cellmate Esco.

"Doesn't that make you feel strange?" he asked.

"Why would I feel strange? I'm not gay."

"But your son is and you accept it," he stated as if he still didn't believe it himself.

"I accept it because I love him unconditionally."

"But he's a homo!"

Shaking my head, I answered, "It's what he chose for his life"

Esco gave me the crazy eyes and said, "If it was my son, I'd kill him."

I've heard that many times, I mused saying, "I used to think like that also but the reality is that I love Drew weather he's gay or straight, it doesn't matter he's my son."

"Eddie, there's something wrong with you," he said.

"What's wrong with me?" I turned facing him.

"Your accepting him like, like it's ok, you know the two of you are going to hell, right?"

Esco also wasn't the first one to remind me that by accepting my son's homosexuality, I'm condemning both of our souls to the eternal hell fire. Looking up at him, sitting on the top bunk with his legs hanging over the side, staring down wide eyed, fearing that I'll be doomed in the afterlife if I didn't forsake Drew and ask for God's forgiveness, I chose my words wisely to make my point.

"You think God is going to punish me for loving my son?" I asked.

"Yeah, and your son's going to hell," he said continuing, "It says so in the bible."

"So I should please God and abandon my son in order to bypass eternity in hell?"

"Yes," he answered fully believing that fable literally.

"But then I'll be living in hell on earth without my son in my life."

"As long as you won't be sinning against God," he chimed back, unconvincing.

Esco's expression was so serious as he pleaded with me in an attempt to save my soul, it was funny and sad at the same time.

"Didn't God create everything that exists?" I asked him to hopefully help him gain a little clarity.

"Yes," he answered.

"Then doesn't that mean he created homosexuality?" I questioned.

"Yes, I mean no!!" he said the look of confusion clearly on his face.

"Which one is it?" I pressed.

"Well... umm, I think."

"What?" I demanded. "What?"

"God created man," he blurted out, "With the choice to choose."

"Oh, so we're given this choice, but if we choose wrong then we're punished for eternity," I said.

"Exactly!" he proudly stated, stepping down the ladder on the end of our beds. Pulling the gray plastic chair that matched the one I was sitting on, flopping down he continued closer to me to defend his indoctrinated beliefs.

"The Bible says that if two men lay together they should be stoned, and I don't mean getting high on pot, what I'm saying is-

"I know what you're saying, the Bible says a lot of things that are of no relevance in this day and age," I pointed out.

"That's why the world is so fucked up!" he stated.

"Esco, that book was written over 2000 years ago, you can't expect it to address all the issues of today, but homosexuality was even an issue so big back then that it's written about in the Torah, Bible, and the Quran."

"And they all say it's a sin," he proclaimed.

"They all also say it's wrong for different races to marry and that slavery is ok. Do you agree with that?" I asked looking him right in the eyes.

"No! But you're taking it out of context," he said.

"How's that?" I demanded.

"Everything's not meant to be so literal," he answered.

"But certain things are?" I questioned.

"Yes, like homosexuality being wrong."

"I've told you, there's no such thing as right and wrong. What's wrong in one person's mind can be totally right to another. Esco, you're not listening-

"Eddie! Don't get started on your 'New Age Guru' thinking crap! That's why you're so burnt out... from reading so many books!" he accused, standing up, storming out of the cell.

As a 24-year-old gangbanger, whose mother is a lesbian and youngest sister recently told him that she was also now dating girls, he was challenged with a somewhat similar, though different, situation as I had in the past. The difference was that the Universe brought him to my cell where he was able to talk about it most of the time, venting his frustrations and wondering how I came to this level of acceptance, that he secretly needed himself.

Later on that evening, after the 10:00 pm lock down count, Esco was ready to touch on the topic once again. Round 2 of Old vs. New thinking began.

"So, Eddie, no matter what your son does, you'll still love him and accept him?" he asked peering over the side of the bed looking down at me, as I read Ernest Holmes, "The Science of Mind."

"Yes," I answered.

"But how can you do that?" he petitioned again.

I closed my book, placing it on the small desk next to the head of my bed, looking up to face Esco, I asked earnestly, "Do you still think your mother loves you?"

"Of course, she loves me! What kind of stupid question is that?" he demanded.

"I'm sure you being in a gang, ending up in Federal prison, isn't the life she wanted for you, right?"

"Of course not."

"But she loves you nonetheless?"

"Yeah," he admitted.

"And do you love her or your sister any less now that you know they're lesbians?" I asked in all seriousness.

"They're just crazy and out of their minds," he stated.

"Well, crazy and out of their minds, does it make you love them any less?"

"No."

"So why is it so difficult for you to comprehend the way I feel about my son?"

"Because we're men for Christ's sake!"

"And I'm man enough to say that I love my son no matter what, so it's all right for you to say you love your mom and sister even though they're eating the cat," I joked laughing to ease the mood.

"Yo! Watch what you're saying about my mom's."

"Esco, you better learn to laugh about that shit or it will keep you crying," I said.

"Don't people look at you as soft?" he asked honestly.

"Living my life concerned with what others think was one of my biggest mistakes. You have to live your life according to terms that make you happy, not what you think makes others happy," I explained.

"I couldn't be happy with my son being a queer, and I'm not happy that my mom and sister think they're lesbians," he said.

"Listen," I told him. "I'm not cheerfully running around, waving a rainbow colored flag pronouncing to the world how proud I am because Drew's gay."

"You might as well be," he fired back. "You're writing a book about it," he finished.

"This book is about how I came to accept his gayness and stopped allowing his sexual preference to define our relationship," I answered back.

"But you would rather Drew be straight, right?"

"Yes, I have no problem admitting that, and I'm sure he would rather have me be a lawyer or doctor so I didn't spend so much of his life locked up. But he doesn't love me less because of the way I choose to live my life, and I can't love him less because of how he chooses to live his."

"You got a good point with that," he admitted.

"What you should think about is calling your mom and sister and let them know that no matter how they choose to live, you still love them," I advised.

"They know that," he replied glancing toward the window then back at me.

"Believe me Esco, you'll make them really happy if they hear you say it."

He bit his lip and nodded his head, and I thought I saw a change in his eyes, so I settled back into my book for the night and let him be alone with the thoughts in his head.

Word quickly spread throughout the prison that I was writing a book about having a gay son. My "Gangster to Guru" self-help manuscripts were commonly requested by other inmates that wanted to get on a positive path towards life, but when "Voice for the Silent Fathers" started being requested, I realized just how important the topic is.

U.S.P. Canaan is one of the most violent federal prisons in America. In 2012, four inmates were murdered, and within the first two months of 2013, one inmate was killed and one correction officer was stabbed to death for close to an hour before any staff even noticed. To say it was a violent place was an understatement, it was more like Gladiator school where only the strongest survived.

Egos were at an all-time high resulting in stabbings every week, but still there was a large majority of the population working to stay in their children's lives. It's difficult enough to confront the issues of having a gay or lesbian child in the free world, in prison it's gargantuan.

During the early morning recreation move, I went outside with a cup of coffee to walk the track. On my second lap, I noticed a friend of mine, Rob, cutting across the green grassy field to catch up with me.

"Eddie!" he called out, "can I spin with you?"

"Of course," I said slowing down, letting him catch up.

After walking the track 2 times I inquired about his family.

"They're doing good," he said, "but there's something I wanted to ask you," he added.

"What's up?" I questioned throwing him a curious glance.

"During the last few visits with my son, I've noticed certain behaviors that... I don't know... just didn't seem normal," he almost choked out the words.

"Yeah," I said.

"And then when I called the house, his mother's talking about how he's standing butt naked in front of her. It's his mother and all but it's just not right."

"How old is he?"

"Thirteen."

"Damn! Butt naked? I thought you would say seven or eight," I sighed, not hiding the surprise in my tone.

"You see what I mean, he's too old to be comfortable standing naked in front of his mother like that."

"Um-hmm," nodding my head already knowing where this was going, fighting off a mental image of the whole scenario, then asking, "Do you think he might be gay?"

"I hope not but I don't know. I know you're writing a book about your situation with your son, and I wanted to read it because I want to be able to keep a relationship with him. I just don't know how you do it," he admitted.

"It ain't as easy as it looks," I answered, "but it's worth it. I'll bring you the first draft at lunch."

"All right, Eddie, I'll meet up with you then," Rob said satisfied with that plan.

A week later walking to the gym to teach the Yoga class, Rob met me on the walkway with my manuscript in his hand and a smile on his face. It forced a smile on my own.

"Come here, Eddie," he said with his arms outstretched pulling me in for a big bear hug.

"What's up, Rob?" I asked returning the hug with a sense of humorist enjoyment that my writing helped him out.

"I loved the book and after all you went through, I had to give you a hug. I know I'll be able to continue to have a relationship with my son if it turns out he's gay," he answered back slapping me.

"That's good, Rob, knowing is half the battle," I joked, "but it means a lot for him even with us in here." I said knowingly.

"Yo, I feel like I know Drew, how is he doing?"

"Last he told me he's still working in McDonald's..."

"At Disney World!" he finished.

"Yeah, he's about to turn twenty, telling me what he thinks I want to hear. All I can do is love him unconditionally."

"That's basically what it comes down to," Rob said agreeing.

"Yeah, but it doesn't mean it's a license for him to take advantage of your acceptable attitude," I told him. "Drew and I have limited boundaries established because I'm still uncomfortable with hearing some of the things he's comfortable with sharing. But he understands and respects that line," I explained.

"If my son turns out to be gay, and I hope he doesn't, those boundaries will be extremely tight," he said as we made our way to the door leading to the building that housed the gym and law library.

"As time passes I expect to be more comfortable with talking about certain things, but right now, I'm taking baby steps," I honestly admitted.

"I just respect that with all you've been through with your son, you stuck it out," Rob said shaking his head.

"Man, that shit ain't even over, he's still a live wire," I admitted thinking about how Drew still has his wild side.

"But he knows you got his back."

"I try to express that to him, but he's at that age where he's mad at the world, so I take it one situation and one day at a time."

"You handled shit a lot better that I would have," he admitted.

"Still, Rob, I mishandled a lot of circumstances because I was afraid to face reality."

Walking down the corridor, I paused waiting for Rob since he got chosen for a random search.

"You teaching your fitness class today?" he asked as we reached the gymnasium doors.

"No, today's Yoga class, you want to try it out?" I asked, adding, "It will be fun and releases a lot of stress."

"Yoga, in a penitentiary?" he said shaking his head. "No, I'll pass for now. Working with my son's issues is enlightening enough for me."

CHAPTER THIRTY-SEVEN

The e-mail computer system was entered into the correctional institution, making communicating with our family and friends a lot easier. It was a relief to see technology catching up with the prison. Another three months passed when I woke up one morning surprised to see Drew's name on the inbox with a message reading:

I'm done with Florida, moving back to New York tonight, wish me luck!

Hitting the reply button, I typed:

Hey Drew, long time since I heard from you. You're moving to New York? How are you getting there? Where will you live? Do you have a job lined up? Send me your cell number. Love, Dad.

Pressing send and logging off the computer, I ran to the phone quickly dialing Jennifer's number to see how realistic Drew's message was.

"Hello, Jennifer," I greeted after she pressed the number five accepting my call.

"Hey Eddie. What's up?" she asked never changing, getting right to the point.

"I got a message from Drew saying he's moving to New York after not hearing from him in months."

"So?" she said.

"What's been going on?"

"Eddie, I don't want nothing to do with your son. He's strung out on drugs again, bringing his sexual lifestyle in the house with no regards for my kids, and it's unhealthy for them!" she said getting herself all worked up.

Was this all a déjà vu? I wondered to myself.

"I understand your concerns, Jennifer, their the same one's I have for my girls. That's why I wouldn't let him move back to New York," I made clear.

"Well, he's an adult now and doesn't listen to nobody but himself," she barked clearly upset, adding, "and that's why he's no longer welcomed in my house."

Damn, I thought, he must really be out of control for real.

"Well, I hope he doesn't think he's going to live with my mother because I'm telling you... that's not happening. Especially after what you just described."

"Like I said, Eddie, I'm done with him. End of story!" she said hanging up in cold Jennifer fashion.

After waiting 30 minutes, I dialed my mother's house.

"Hellooo, Daddy!" Alexa answered with the innocent voice of a 10-year-old.

"Hey Princess. How was school?"

"Fine. I got another 100 on my math test," she proudly let me know.

"That's great! I need to talk to Grams; it's important."

"Grams is right here," she said passing my mother the phone.

"Hey Son."

"Mom, have you heard from Drew recently?"

"No, it's been a few months, why? Is he ok?" She asked.

"Yes and no," I answered. "I'm not sure. I just received a message from him telling me he's moving to New York. Did you have anything to do with this?"

"First I'm hearing of it, Ed. Where's he staying?"

"I don't know. He just said he's leaving tonight. You know how he is, says very little and knows it will worry me a lot. I spoke to Jennifer, and Ma trust me, he's in no condition to be living at your house according to what she said."

"I understand your concerns, Ed. If I hear from him, I'll let you know," she assured me.

Alexa was enjoying Drew's company, anxious to talk to me when I called later that evening.

"Hi, Daddy!"

"There's that voice that lifts my spirits! How's your day sweetheart?"

"Good we're cooking with Mom."

"Wish I could be there."

"Me, too," she replied then asked, "Daddy, why does Drew talk like he's a girl?"

This little girl, I thought, she's always saying what's on her mind. After a slight pause I told her, "He's just a little different in some ways, princess."

"Oh well, Dad, I think it's because he's gay. Yeah, I'm pretty sure that's it, Drew's gay."

This was coming from my ten-year-old innocent angel, forcing reality on me. After another slight pause due to my thoughts spinning a bit, I simply replied, "Yes baby, that's why. Can I talk with Mom?" I asked wanting to change the conversation.

"Sure," she answered sounding proud that she cleared any questions in my mind as to why Drew speaks the way he does.

"Hey Honey," Maria answered.

"Hear you're in the kitchen."

"Yep, cooking with your three daughters," she joked.

"Very funny. Everything all right?"

"Yeah, basically in the house all day."

"Drew keeping it cool?" I asked.

"Pssst, Drew is Drew, but nothing too crazy. He's been a trip to have around, but he's too wild and I'm telling you, he wants to live here I can tell."

"It's just a visit for the weekend," I assured her.

"I know, Kelly's picking him up tomorrow afternoon, but I can tell he's going to try to move here the first chance he gets, and I'm not exposing the girls to all his drama."

"Don't worry it's not happening. I'll call tomorrow."

Getting off the phone, I walked over to the cell of my friend Paradise and shared my concerns about Drew being at the house doing something crazy while he's there.

Paradise has been in prison over 18 years and at 36 years old, he's basically grown up in the bureau of prisons. Entering his cell, the strong scent of Egyptian musk oil emanating from a little rag stuck in his vent engulfed my senses.

"Guess what Alexa just let me know?" I said pulling out one of his gray plastic chairs identical to the ones in my cell.

"Oh, you just got off the phone? What did she say?" he asked hoisting himself out of his bunk, placing the "Twilight" novel he was reading on his desk.

"She let me know that Drew's gay."

"Oh shit!" he said with a big smile, and then continued, "She's only ten right? That's crazy but it's a new world out there Eddie. This generation, it's like being gay is in style."

"If it is, Drew is defiantly the trend setter, because things have really changed over the years." I said.

"Eddie, that gay shit stays in the news with them wanting to get married and all," he stated.

"I know. I just didn't expect my daughter to understand what being gay is at ten years old."

"With the internet, there's nothing these kids don't know."

"Please don't remind me. Drew got mad for me asking him to tone down his gayness."

"What did you expect? It's who he is."

"No, it's not who he is," I shot back.

"Well, it's how he identifies himself," he replied.

"That's true, but it's only a small aspect of who he is, and he's so much more than just being gay."

Standing up from his bed, Paradise turned on the hot water in his porcelain white sink, letting it run while grabbing a bag of coffee out of his steel gray locker.

"You want a cup of Joe?"

"Nah, I'm good," I answered.

"Eddie, you know Drew's more than his gayness as you call it," he said while making quotations signs in the air with both hands, "but he might not know that yet. You got to remember he's still young."

"True, but he's just so extra with that shit and it's frustrating."

"Frustrating to you, out there it's just what it is. Look at all the grown ass men in here still searching for themselves."

"I know you're right," I admitted.

We spoke for another ten minutes then I left to get ready to lock in for the night. The following morning was Sunday, the day I normally relax but I decided to go outside and run the track for thirty minutes, do some cardio for another hour and then came back inside to take a shower.

Once I got myself ready and checked my e-mail, I was happy to see there wasn't an emergency message from Maria or my mother telling me to call. I began cutting onions and peppers for the nachos to eat during the afternoon of watching the N.F.L. football games. I had plans to call the house during half-time.

At the house, Maria made plans with Drew to go to the local Subway.

"Call your Aunt, Drew, and have her meet us at the sub-shop. I am going to the gym straight from there," Maria said.

"Ok, I don't know what came over me Maria, I just have this crazy craving for a hero with the works."

"Say good-bye to Grams and your sisters. I'll be in the truck."

Ten minutes later, pulling up to the Subway Drew told her, "You know my father really pissed me off."

"Why, what did he do?" Maria asked at the same time turning off the engine.

"He has the nerve, always telling me to tone down the way I am."

"He just worries about how the girls interpret the way you are," Maria defended.

"The way I am?" he questioned shocked with surprise.

"Yes, Drew, no matter how feminine you act, you're still their brother, which can be confusing to the girls being so young."

"There's nothing confusing about it sweetheart, it's the reality of life!" he snapped back as he stepped out the truck, heading into the Subway with Maria shaking her head following behind.

"Oh, this air condition feels magnificent!" Drew announced in his tumultuous girlish tone, attracting all the attention from the other customers. He continued, "And look at this gorgeous man! You ready to take my order?" he asked the young guy behind the counter who hesitated and asked, "What could I get you?"

"You!!" Drew roared looking him straight in the eyes.

"Ummm, excuse me?" he asked clearly embarrassed.

"Drew just order your food!" Maria demanded.

"I am! God! I'll take a foot-long chicken and cheese with the works, honey."

"Can you make two of those please with two large sodas," Maria interrupted. "What kind of drink do you want, Drew?"

"What's gotten into you?" he asked.

"What-do-you-want-to drink?" Maria emphasized through clenched teeth.

"A 7-Up."

"And two 7-Ups, please. We'll take that to go," she told the employee taking their order.

"Let's eat in here with the comfortable air condition," Drew whined.

"No! I'm eating in the truck."

"Why?"

"Drew, not now!" she barked.

Rolling his neck, sucking his teeth twirling around, Drew took a seat in one of the booths as the order was prepared then packed in plastic bags and paid for by Maria.
Walking past Drew without saying a word, Drew rolled his eyes again, stomped his feet on the brown ceramic tile floor, letting out a loud sigh and followed her out the door. Once in the passenger seat of the truck he asked, "What's the matter with you, girl?"

"The way you were acting with that young guy in there Drew!"

"What? I gave him a compliment."

"Drew, you embarrassed him and me!"

"Oh, I guess I should have toned it down, right?"

"Yes, Drew, everybody doesn't live in your world, that guy could have gotten upset and jumped across the counter."

"And he would have gotten what he was looking for too!" he shot back defensively.

"Listen to you. I have friends that are gay Drew, but they don't push it on everyone they meet. You want people to respect you but you have to respect other people. That display in there was disrespectful."

"Please, Maria, you're just another person that don't understand me."

"No, I guess I don't because that behavior was rude."

Just as she said that, Drew's Aunt Kelly pulled up alongside the truck, in her midnight blue four-door Corolla.

"Well, look who it is, right on time. You have a good day, Maria," he said getting out grabbing his bag of Subway.

Maria waved at his Aunt Kelly, who waved back as Drew climbed in her passenger seat.

"I really felt bad for that Subway worker," Maria said to me after explaining what occurred when I called that night.

"Well, there's nothing we can do."

"I'm glad the girls weren't with me," Maria admitted.

"Me, too," I said.

"I'm sorry, Eddie, but I'm not going to have him acting just any kind of way around our girls. I know he's your son but if you would have seen the way he was acting, I don't know what you would have done."

"Listen, he'll probably do him for a few months. You made it through the weekend so don't worry too much," I said in an attempt to keep her calm.

But with Drew and his antics, with him living on Long Island, I was the one that was worrying.

CHAPTER THIRTY-EIGHT

Three rapid taps on the front door, two weeks later in the late night, Drew revealed himself standing soaking wet from the down pouring rain, carrying a black over stuffed duffel bag, wearing a blue and white Yankees cap pulled low covering his forehead. His water logged clothes dripping a small puddle on the oak wood floor of my mother's living room, more evidence of him having been out doors for an extended amount of time, he was saturated from head to toe.

"Grams! I need a place to stay," he announced taking off his hat, shaking out his drenched hair.

"Oh my gosh, honey, let me get you something to dry off with," she answered ushering him further inside.

"Aunt Kelly kicked me out," he said as she went to the linen closet, returning with a thick green cotton bath towel.

"Here, dry yourself off before you get sick. Tell me what happened."

"That bitch accused me of stealing from her! Whenever she's high she gets all paranoid, thinking everyone's out to get her," he complained while peeling out of the soggy shirt he was wearing under a gray windbreaker jacket.

"Drew, watch your language and keep it down. The girls are sleeping. Why would she accuse you?"

"Who knows, Grams, she's all strung out and crazy! That's why they took her kids."

"Well, get yourself into some dry clothes, I'll make you some tea."

"Where should I put my stuff?" he asked.

"You'll have to stay in the living room, I'll make you a bed on the couch after I put the water on."

As my mother explained the circumstances to me the following morning, I listened, pressing my lips together, shaking my head anticipating hearing Maria's mouth with her 'I told you so' attitude.

"Mom, you have to find him somewhere to live."

"I'm already looking up listings, Ed."

"It's fucked up, Ma, but he can't get comfortable there."

"Language please" she said.

"Sorry, but he's too much of a live wire to be at the house."

"I'm sure I'll find something for him," she assured me.

"Ok, where is he now?"

"Eating lunch with Nia and Alexa."

"Where's Maria?"

"Upstairs."

"Let me talk with her first."

"One second."

These fifteen minute calls make it extremely difficult to deal with complex situations. I signaled Paradise to bring my plastic chair. Sitting down, leaning my head on the base of the phone booth, I was not looking forward to hearing Maria's mouth.

"Hello?" she said.

"Hey, I hear you have company."

"Didn't I tell you he would end up staying here?"

"He won't be there long, my mother will find him a place to rent," I tried to assure her.

"Drew's smoking like chimney."

"In the house?"

"No, out on the front porch but still I don't like that shit around the girls."

"It's temporary," I said.

"I'm not saying anything else, you already know how I feel, Eddie. I'm going to see what your mother does and make my choice with the girls because this is her house, and he's her grandson."

"Calm down, Maria, stop being so dramatic, it's not that serious."

"Not that serious for you because you're not here to have to deal with this shit! I am!!" she barked.

"All right, let me talk to Drew."

"Hold on."

Glancing at my Timex digital watch, I had about five minutes left to talk with Drew. Hearing Maria call him to the phone, I mentally prepared myself for what I would hear.

"Hiya Dad," he enthusiastically answered.

"Hey Drew, Grams told me what happened at your aunt's."

"Yeah, that bitch is tripping."

"Was that the only problem the two of you had?" I asked.

"It's been little things here and there but to accuse me of stealing money, when I work my ass off earning my own money, is fucked up and I refuse to live with a bitch like that."

"Drew, easy with the language."

"Sorry, she just has my blood boiling."

"Grams said she's checking on a place for you to rent."

"Yeah, we're going to look at some spots tomorrow."

He sounded cool with finding a new place to live which I was happy for because I thought he might start to argue with me about moving back with my mother.

"Well, just don't bring any drama to the house while you're there Drew."

"I won't, Dad."

"You know my situation is stressful enough, we're all dealing with a lot right now."

"I know, Dad," he said adding, "you being locked up has had a big effect on me also you know."

"I know that, so we don't need to add any more to it."

"I said I won't, Dad," he replied with a heavy sigh.

"And Drew-

"I know already you want me to tone down my gayness?"

"No," I said even though it was exactly what I was going to say. "I just wanted to remind you that I love you."

"I love you too, Dad, and no worries, we're all going to a party tonight at the new family's house on the block."

"All right, this phone's going to cut off so have a good time."

"Ok, bye!"

Regardless what conditions Drew was in, my mother wanted him to stay at the house, I could tell. But with the girls living there it was like she had to pick between her grandchildren adding to her frustrations. After Jennifer described his behaviors at her house, there was just no way he would have the opportunity to do that around my mother and the girls... or so I thought.

The following morning, I called to keep the pressure on, to make sure that plans for looking at rental properties were still on track. It was Nia who answered my call.

"Hi Princess!"

"Hi Daddy. Ummm, Daddy?"

I could hear in her voice something was on her mind as I asked, "Yes baby?"

"Drew was dancing very inappropriately last night."

"He was," I said with a cool tone keeping myself calm.

"Yes, he was taking off his clothes and Alexa was crying. Mommy's very upset."

"Is mommy awake sweetheart?" I asked.

"Yeah."

"Let me talk to her to find out what happened."

Hearing my five year-old use the term inappropriately when describing her older brother's behaviors, ignited the onset of an all too regular migraine headache from anticipating the bitch fest of complaints I was about to hear from Maria.

"Hello?" she answered with a sharp hostile temper.

"Nia told me there was-

"Your son is out of control!"

"I heard."

"No you don't understand, he got drunk, started dancing like some slutty stripper, disrespecting your mother when she tried to calm him down and was disrespecting me! Alexa was crying, your mother is upset, and I'm just not going to deal with this bull shit!" she roared.

"Ok, ok, calm down, Maria."

"Don't tell me to calm down, you weren't there, you're never here!" she reminded me, something she was been doing more and more.

"Put my mother on the phone please."

"Yeah, talk with her!"

My head was throbbing filled with images of Drew dancing bare chest, swinging his shirt in the air in the middle of the party, pushing my mother away, Alexa in tears, Nia scared...

"Good morning, Ed."

"Is it mom? I'm hearing about last night and it doesn't sound so good to me."

"It wasn't, not at all."

"You see why I said what I said."

"Yes."

"Where is Drew?"

"Hung over, asleep on the couch."

"Wake his ass up and make those appointments."

"That's what I'm about to do because after what he showed me last night, staying here is out of the question," she said.

As upset as I was that he acted out, the experience convinced my mother of what I already knew. There was no doubt that she was now on the same page as far as Drew not living at the house until he's willing to clean up his act. It's hard loving my son so much and feeling so helpless while he's on this destructive path.

He's like a drunk driver, speeding down the highway at night with no lights on. It's inevitable that he's going to crash, I can only hope that he survives the wreck because it's imminent. What I didn't expect was that the crash would happen later that day.

Five heavy thumps, knocking at 4:30 pm caused Alexa to run to the front door.

"Mom!! The police are here!" she yelled.

"What!!" Maria shouted from her room upstairs.

"The police are here knocking at the door!" Alexa repeated with a shout.

Nia came dashing down the stairs, jumping on the couch, pushing aside the curtains, pressing her face against the window to see the two uniformed officers waiting. Marching down the stairs, Maria gave a quick look out the same window leaning over the top of Nia, then moved to answer the door with Alexa and Nia following and standing quietly at her side as she answered the door.

"Can I help you?" she asked.

"We're looking for Drew Romero," the first officer standing closest to the door announced in an even calm tone.

"What's this about?"

"Is he here Mrs..."

"Mrs. Wright, I'm his mother," she said.

"The Drew we're looking for is nineteen years old, you look a little too young to be his mother," the second officer injected.

"I'm his step-mother and again what's this about?"

"Is he here, Mrs. Wright?" the first office asked again.

"No, he's not but if you answer my question I may be able to help you locate him," she offered.

Both officers took a second to look at one another and then when the second officer gave a nod of his head to his partner, the first officer explained, "We have a warrant for his arrest on a domestic issue."

"A domestic issue?" Maria repeated.

"Yes, it seems he had an incident with his aunt," the same officer explained.

"Ok, give me a minute to make a call to see where he is."

"Sure, we'll appreciate the help."

Closing the door, leaving the officers standing on the front porch, Maria walked into the kitchen to give my mother a call.

"Jean!"

"Hi, honey," she answered.

"The police are here looking for Drew!"

"Oh my god, why?"

"They said it's about his aunt, a domestic issue and they have a warrant," she explained.

"Ok... oh God...Ummm, tell them we'll be there in about half an hour."

"All right," Maria said.

Hanging up the phone, the police went and sat in their patrol car to wait after Maria relayed the message.

"Drew why are the police at the house looking for you?" my mother asked as she drove from Patchogue, where she just put a security deposit down for an apartment they found within walking distance from his job.

"I guess Kelly called them, that bitch!" he pouted.

"Are you telling me everything that happened?'

"Yes, Grams, she accused me of stealing, we argued, I packed my stuff and left," he explained.

"Now the police are involved Drew, you'll have to go with them, but I'll be there to bail you out whatever it is."

"I can't believe she called the cops. Let me call my mother," he said.

Passing Drew her phone, my mother rubbed her head in frustration, worrying as she continued driving towards the house.

"Mom?"

"Yes, Drew?" Jennifer answered.

"Aunt Kelly called the cops on me!" he cried.

"I know, she called and told me."

"Why?" he asked.

"You know why Drew, now you have to deal with it, there's nothing I can do."

"Can't you call her and tell her not to press charges?" he pleaded.

"She's not going to drop the charges, and I'm not getting involved. Your grown, deal with it."

"Fine!" he yelled snapping the phone closed.

"I guess I'm going to jail, Grams," he said leaning back, hugging himself with watery eyes.

"You'll be fine, Drew, it will only be a few hours. Let me stop and get you something to eat first."

"But the cops are at the house."

"They can wait," she said pulling into a row of stores with a deli where she was able to buy him a chicken cutlet with cheese and a soda.

Forty-five minutes later, they pulled up to the house where the police took Drew into their custody.

"Once he's processed he'll be able to be bailed out from Riverhead County Jail. It will take about two to three hours," the first cop that knocked on the door explained to my mother.

"Ok, thank you," she said, then yelling, "I'll be there to bail you out. Don't worry!" to Drew who was sitting in the back of the patrol car. As they pulled away, the girls waved as he was looking down at the floor of the police cruiser shaking his head.

This time it was Alexa who answered the phone when I called later that evening.

"Hi, Daddy!"

"Hey sweetheart."

"It's been a very exciting day with lots of drama," she informed me.

"I already heard about last night."

"Nope, I said today, Dad, today! But I better let mom explain it to you."

I knew it was something big right then since Alexa loves to tell me what's going on any chance she has.

After Maria filled me in on the day's events, I got off the phone so I could call back when Drew was home. It was another thirty minutes as I contemplated what to say. This isn't the life I ever wanted for my son, knowing that after your first arrest, the second one comes that much easier, making you start falling into a pattern of being in and out of jail for the rest of your life.

"Mom, what's going on? Did you bail him out?"

"Yes, he's smoking outside on the porch."

"How is he?"

"He's all right. A little shaken up but maybe it's something he needed."

"What was he charged with?" I asked.

"Well, it was more than an argument, he got physical with Kelly and he was charged with assault."

"Assault! He hit her?"

"He said he just pushed her and that she's exaggerating to get him in trouble."

"Well, it's working. Any luck with an apartment?" I questioned.

"Yep, he'll move in tomorrow."

"Good, let me talk to him."

"Ok, hold on."

What I expected to say to Drew got wiped from my mind now that I heard the charges. I also knew he wouldn't be receptive to another speech that I was certain my mother gave him on the 45-minute ride from being bailed out from the jail.

"Hello?" he answered in a low hush tone.

"You all right, Drew?"

"Yeah."

"Listen, I'm not glad you had to experience going to jail, but your mother told me you got physical with her and I didn't want to believe it, now your charged with assault on Kelly."

"But Dad-

"Hold on, Drew, let me finish. I don't care how feminine you are, you're still a man and there's never a reason to put your hands on a woman."

"Uh-huh," he said.

"I asked you not to bring drama to the house, now look. Grams is worried to death and so am I."

"I didn't know Kelly called the police," he whined.

"Maybe so, but all that shit at the party was too much."

"I was drunk."

"I already know, and you're too young to be drinking."

"Mom's been letting me drink since I was sixteen," he defended.

"Fuck what your mother let you do, you need to clean up your act and until you do, just popping up at Gram's house thinking you're going to do whatever you want 'ain't happening,' I said raising my voice with a harsh tone.

"Uh-huh," he moaned.

I took a deep breath to calm myself down because I was pissed. "You had a rough day. Tomorrow you're moving into your apartment, we paid the security and first month's rent so don't fuck it up."

"I won't."

"Damn, Drew, I hate having to be hard on you like this but I know your wilding out now."

"I'm fine, Dad."

"No you're not! You need to sober up and stay out of trouble. I'll call to check up on you."

"All right," he said, and we got off the phone.

With his living arraignments taken care of for a month, I called Mimi who put him on her cellular plan and brought him a phone so we could stay in contact. He was walking distance to his job and had a comfortable place to live on his own. I just wished he would accept our offer to get counseling or rehab but he wasn't at that stage in life where he was open for that at all. This left me with that quiet ever present ticking of a clock to strike zero, waiting the next episode in Drew's life to explode.

CHAPTER THIRTY-NINE

My mother was back in full inspector mode during the first month Drew spent in his apartment. Now Drew had the Gestapo on his case constantly, checking up on him at his job, calling his phone, and taking him out to dinner, which served 2 agendas. The first, just spending time catching up with her grandson, but it was also a means for one of her classic interrogation tactics to get a feel of what was going on.

"Are you putting money aside for your rent that's coming up?" she grilled as soon as they got settled at their table.

"Of course, Grams, I got it covered," he answered giving his attention to the menu of the Blue Moon Diner.

"I'm proud of you, Drew. I know it's not easy being young and on your own," she commented.

"It's not my first time being on my own, Grams, I'm used to it."

After ordering their meals and polite conversation, his Grandmother continued her probe.

"You have your court hearing at the end of next week."

"I know."

"I'll pick you up because you don't want to be late."

"I can get myself there," he said.

"I'm sure you can, honey, but I took the day off so it will be no trouble," she replied with a tone that assured him it wasn't a suggestion. She was taking him.

"Fine, Grams," he said knowing she wasn't going to accept no for an answer.

Two days later at 1:30 am Drew called my mother's house.

"Grams, I need Aunt Mimi's cell number," he demanded in a high excited tone.

"Why? What going on?" she asked in a half sleep half-awake voice.

"I lost my phone during a fight with some bitch ass mother fucker at the club," he whined between deep pouts.

Charged with a jolt of energy, standing her right out of bed after what she was told.

"Jesus! Are you all right? Where are you now?"

"I'm fine, on my way home but I just can't live without my phone," he cried.

"Drew, you're out on bail, getting into fights, that's not good," she said turning the reading lamp on next to her bed.

"Don't worry, Grams, I got this. Can I just have her number."

Rushing off the phone once he had Mimi's number, my mother was left with another sleepless night of worry.

"I don't know what to do, Ed, the path he's on is dangerous," she said later that day when I called.

"I know it's hard but until he's ready to change his life, there's really not much we can do," I explained.

"What if the police are looking for him because of that fight? What if it's something other than a fight? What if-

"Don't beat yourself up with the what if's, Ma," I injected, "deal with what we know and half of what he tells us," I warned.

"He was extremely hesitant when I insisted on taking him to court."

"Because he knows you're going to get the full story."

"I just don't want him going to jail."

"It's Family Court, Ma, there's nothing to really worry about. Is Jennifer coming to the hearing?" I asked already anticipating the answer.

"No one mentioned anything to me," she said.

"Everything will work itself out mom, don't worry. Let me talk with the girls."

Drew appeared in Family Court along with his grandmother standing at his side; like the hired gun I've grown to know so well. Walking in the court room wearing a neck brace, carrying a stack of medical documents, leaning on her lawyer, Drew's Aunt Kelly stared them both down with a vengeful look, preparing to go to war.

A wave of heat flashed through my body as my temper was about to lose control. Knuckles turning white from tightening my grip on the phone...*Woooooo saaaaaahhhh* I thought, to remain calm and in control. *Woooooo saaaaaaahhhh.*

"So you're just going to throw Drew to the wolves by abandoning him?" I said throwing my Zen philosophy of "no conflict" aside.

"Who the fuck are you to talk about abandoning him? You disowned Drew once you met Maria. Abandonment, please mother fucker you spent most his life in prison, and you have the nerve to judge me! Fuck you, Eddie!! Fuck you!!"

Her second statement hit a sore spot because it was true that I was in prison for most of Drew's life. Still I managed to keep a little calm because I knew this wasn't going to help Drew's situation at all.

Choosing my words carefully to make it sound less like a request, I pleaded for Drew's sake, "Listen, Jennifer, we've both made mistakes in our past but we need to do what's best for our son now."

"There's nothing I can do," she automatically shot back, adding, "Your mother was and is always there for you with all your troubles so what's the problem now?"

That statement pissed me off. Fuck the Buddhism, new age, "keep the universe in harmony" state of thinking, it was just no use.

"My mother is there for me because I'm her son! The way you're Drew's mother! If my Aunt had me arrested for anything and was doing everything in her power to put me in jail, my mother would have beat her ass until the charges were dropped. I'm only asking you to call Kelly and you're being a bitch about that!" I screamed into the phone.

"I don't have to explain anything to you, I'm done with this conversation!"

Click.

CHAPTER FORTY

Contacting Drew was a rigorous task since he had yet to replace the phone he claimed he couldn't live without. My mother happened to pick him up for one of her dinners on the first of the month. At the Olive Garden restaurant, sitting with trimmed manicured eye brows, and freshly painted cherry red nails, Drew grabbed one of the warm sesame covered bread sticks that the waiter placed on the table as he said, "You should try this new shade for your nails, Grams, it's hot!"

"No, thanks, I like neutral colors. I'm too old for anything hot," she replied with a gentle smile.

"Please, Grams, you're still young, and if you take some of my fashion tips, I'll get you a man," he promised between bites.

"A man is the last thing on my mind, Drew. Did you pay your landlord today?"

"Of course, in full before I left for work this morning," he answered without batting an eye.

"That's good, honey. I was a little worried. But you're being responsible with your job and priorities. I'm so proud of you," she said.

"Yep, doing what I gots to do," he announced, twisting his neck with each syllable spoken.

*

Drew's landlord called my mother 2 days later complaining that he hadn't received anything towards the rent.

Drew ignored her calls. He wasn't at work when she passed by and she didn't hear from him for another two weeks when he decided to call her.

"Grams, I need your help," he pleaded as soon as she answered the phone causing her a scare, thinking he was in some type of danger.

"What, Drew? Where are you, where have you been?"

"Busy, busy, busy taking care of this and that," he said.

"Like what, Drew, because your landlord called and..."

"Don't worry about that, Grams, I'll explain when you come help me move my stuff. Can you help me?" he asked.

"Move it where?"

"To my friend's apartment where I'll be staying."

"Where are you now?"

"At work until 5:00 pm, can you pick me up then?"

"I'll be there," she answered as he knew she would.

After reading my mother's e-mail message updating me on what's going on with Drew, I called her cell phone at 5:30 pm knowing she would be with him.

"Mom, what's up?"

"Hey Son, how you doing?"

"Fine," I said. "Are you with Drew?"

"Yeah, he's loading the last of his stuff in the trunk. Hold on," she said passing Drew the phone.

"Hey Daddy!" he answered excited and just as flamboyant as ever.

"Drew, what the hell is going on?" I asked in a calm tone.

"Just too much to discuss now, Dad."

"Too much to... Drew, why didn't you pay your rent?" I asked raising my voice.

"I've been spending money like I got it," he sang more than spoke as if it was the hook of a new rap song.

"What about your rent?" I emphasized.

"I needed to buy clothes but no worries I got a place to stay."

"You need a place to live! Save your money because crashing on someone's couch gets played out fast."

"Don't worry I got this. I'll prove it to you," he replied.

"You don't have to prove anything to me, just to yourself," I repeated what seemed to be a mantra between us.

"Ok, Dad, here talk to Grams," he said classically rushing me off the phone.

"Mom?"

"Yes, Ed."

"He sounds erratic," I said.

"He's all over the place," then she whispering, "I think he's high on something."

"Take him wherever he's going and tell him when he's ready for a rehab to call," I bluntly stated.

"I know, I'll push it, Ed."

"Don't give him any money, he'll use it to get high."

"I won't, you just keep calm and stay out of trouble. I can hear you're upset," she said.

"Ma, everything in here is fine, out there is where all the stress and problems are!"

"Ok Son, call me tonight."

After years of struggling with having a homosexual son, I've evolved to praying for Drew to act like a normal gay man. *Am I asking God for too much?* I wondered to myself. It was so easy for things to take a drastic turn for the worst, like it did with me when not considering the unforeseen consequences of my actions. Right then, Drew was a live wire, living la-Vida-loca, refusing to accept any type of professional help because he didn't think he needed it so didn't want it.

I sent Drew long e-mail messages explaining how lessons in life continuously repeat themselves until we take heed to learn from them. Those lessons get more strenuous each time around, and I used my life and the circumstances I've been in as an example. Even though I know Drew wasn't trying to hear anything like that now, I still sent it, letting him know that I loved him.

It was the pot calling the kettle black, telling him to get his life on track while I sat in a Federal Penitentiary, but I was his father and that was never going to change regardless if I was in prison or not, and I made clear that how he chose to live his life wouldn't change that either. Leave it to Drew to put my words to the test just a few months after moving with his new friends.

*

Drew re-established himself back in New York, continuing to hold down his job as a cashier, while being comfortable crashing with his friends at their apartment. My mother continued checking up on him, interviewing the couple he was living with and made sure that if he wanted to sober up, our offer for help was always there. Drew would quickly change the topic any time she brought up his need for rehab, but the important thing was he knew we cared.

He defiantly started embracing his feminine attributes in how he was dressing, and I could hear it also in his voice, not only the tone but in his choice of words and how he would express himself. Yet the deepness of his voice that he inherited from me was the one thing that he couldn't change.

Picking up the receiver to call yet another one of his cell numbers, saying a routine prayer asking for a reasonable sane conversation as I took a deep breath, slowly pushing each button.

"Hellooo, Daddy," came the extra girlish voice over the phone that I've mastered to ignore.

"Hey! How's life been treating you?" I asked somewhat afraid of the answer.

"Oh, it's good! I've been busy with friends going clubbing in Manhattan where there's just so much to do for people in my scene," he said sounding hyped up and excited.

"That's good, how's work?"

"It's a job for now but I'm looking to do more, like getting myself a reality show. Everyone says I should do it so I am. Plus my 21st birthday is coming up and I'm planning to rent a club to celebrate."

"Drew, you turned twenty just two weeks ago," I pointed out.

"Yeah, but this is my year and it's going to be such a big event that I have to start making the arrangements now," he answered like it all made perfect sense.

"You still living in the same place?"

"Yeap, it's a cool spot."

"Don't you think you should get your own apartment before planning to rent a club?"

"Why can't you just ever support me? God! You always have some negative shit to say," he spat.

"What's negative? I'm just suggesting you make sure you have a good place to live before you spend money on things you don't need," I tried to explain in a calm tone.

"Don't worry about it, I'll get it done," he shot back.

"Do you have a plan 'B', if the reality show doesn't come through?" I asked.

"I don't need a plan 'B' it's going to happen, and I don't need your negative energy right now. Call me when you're not so moody and more supportive!"

Click!

This son of mine didn't sound like he was dealing with reality, yet he wanted a reality show. I wasn't expecting him to have his life mapped out, he was too young for that. But a reasonable idea of going to school, or anything else besides just the hopes of landing a reality show was all I was asking for. This wasn't the only conversation where Drew rambled about his big plans and ideas.

Anytime I would try to inject some rational question to his attention, it was perceived as if I wasn't supporting him. There was nothing I could really do or say. Drew was an adult and I had to accept the fact that I was his his life to live. It got to the point that I began to prepare myself for the possibility that he might be contemplating having a sex change operation. Of course, I never discussed it with him for fear of planting the seed but it just seemed plausible considering his behavior and how extreme he'd always been. I guess I was to blame for that since I was an extreme gangster, and he was an extremely gay man!

Since mentally I already prepared myself for that scenario, when I called the following week, I handled the news of his latest episode extremely well.

"How you doing, Drew?" I asked when I called.

"Oh, I'm doing great actually super super hyped," he answered speaking extra fast.

Automatically I suspected he was high on something, Drew always sounds excited but today was different, there was something he wanted me to know.

"Well, calm down, because when you're all stirred up and jittery, it's hard for me to keep up with you."

"That's cause you're getting old, Dad," he jibbed.

"Old? Yeah okay, what's going on?"

"It's just that I'm feeling great, and my head is all big because I nailed my performance last night."

"Performance?" I repeated with a slight hesitation asking, "What kind of performance?" again while not really wanting to know.

"You're not ready to know that. Dad" he said as if reading my mind. "Just know it was a performance!"

Hyper speed images, flashed in my mind of Drew promenading at some homosexual strip club, wearing black leather tights with chrome chains dangling from his nipples down to his waist, voguing to the sounds of Y.M.C.A. It was hard to catch my breath -feeling myself perspiring during the momentary silence over the phone that seemed like forever- before I forced myself to say what I knew he wanted to hear.

"Drew, there is nothing you could do that would shock me to the point that I would stop loving you."

"I know," he said.

"So if you would like to tell me the type of performance it was, that's fine. If not, then that's fine also," I said with hopes of him not wanting to tell me, but hearing him breathing a sigh of relief, I knew he just wanted to hear it was all right to tell me, and tell me he did.

"Last night, I dressed up in drag as Nicki Minaj, performing one of her songs at a gay club with a packed house!" His voice was rising as he got increasingly excited. "I got paid, they gave me free drinks, and everyone said I was the best out of all the performers," he proudly let me know.

"Really?" was all I could muster up to say.

"Yeap, and this is going to open the door for a new career of performing in the city. I already have a booking for a major club in Manhattan."

Dear reader,

You have to be wondering what I could have possibly been thinking upon hearing this new revelation, well let me share with you that my first thought was *I would never be able to look at or listen to anything by Nicki Minaj.* My next thought was more of a question...

What could Drew possibly be expecting me to say? Congratulations Son! Make me proud, that's my boy! No, I just didn't have that in me. This wasn't the plan 'B' I was expecting. I wanted to scream at the top of my lungs "What the fuck are you doing you crazy son of a bitch!" But that wouldn't change a thing.

I simply responded by saying, "If that's what you choose to do, and it makes you happy, then I'm happy for you."

"Oh, it does make me happy Dad, and I'm so lucky to have a father that understands," he said all happy and proud.

The fact is, I didn't understand at all. I didn't have a clue but I didn't have to, he was my son.

"Did you speak to your mother? Does she know about this? I asked.

"Hell, yeah, she knew and called me before the show to wish me good luck," he lavishly boasted.

Why wasn't I the least bit surprised?

We talked a little more and I politely got off the phone while holding the vision of Jennifer pointing at me, laughing herself to tears at me hearing about this new career move of my one and only son. But after the initial shock subsided, I was the one that started laughing to myself. It wasn't one of those laughs that lead to me crying tears of misfortune. No, this was just a genuine authentic laugh.

If my son wanted to dress up as a woman, singing and dancing on stage for all the world to see, so be it. I don't have to understand it or agree with it. The fact is, there is nothing he could do that would stop me from loving him.

CHAPTER FORTY-ONE

"What's up little brother?" Mimi asked after accepting my call.

"Nothing much, working on my appeal and staying out of the way of this prison drama. What's going on?"

"Taking care of the boys and finalized the divorce papers, thank God," she answered.

"How are my nephews?"

"They're getting big, keeping me busy."

"That's good," I said.

Mimi moved to California to attend San Diego University, fell in love with the weather, and vowed never to move back east. Twenty-three years later, she was sticking to that promise. Regardless of living on the opposite side of the United States, we still stayed close. The entertainment business kept me in L.A. on a regular basis so we always hung out for a few days whenever I was in town.

"I've been waiting for you to call," she said.

"Why, what's up?"

"Your son!"

"Please Mimi, you're talking about his performance right?"

"No, he calls claiming he found out he had a sister his age. Of course, I denied it because you were so whipped by his mother," she said with laugh.

"Yeah whatever, so what the hell is he talking about?"

"Drew insisted it's true and that he would prove it to me, sending a picture of my mysterious niece."

"Uh-huh," I said taking a deep breath that I held while she continued. "So, I get an e-mail with the picture, and its Drew dressed up as a girl, calling himself Draya!" She busted out laughing as she finished her sentence causing me to join right along with her since it was laughing that I discovered was the best way for me to mentally deal with these ongoing sagas. Regaining my composure, I said, "Drew is constantly doing some outlandish shit, Mimi, it's crazy but I think it's a cry for help."

"He needs some type of counseling, and I told him he's crazy but he just agreed with me," she said.

"You know they offered him a plea of only one-year probation, and he turned it down!" I said.

"No, he didn't Eddie" she said gasping in a breath of air.

"Yes, he did and guess why?"

"Tell me."

I took a deep breath, thinking about what Drew told me last time we spoke.

"Since he's turning 21 this year he can't be on probation because he has to be able to drink."

"Oh, God," Mimi muttered.

"Yeah, and it would also require him to have a psychological evaluation."

"He needs one," she said.

"You think?" I replied sarcastically. Continuing I said, "When I told him to take the plea, he said it would require him to have too much self-control."

"That's not a bad thing," she said.

"That's what I told him but he wasn't hearing me."

"It's his choice to make," she admitted.

"I know but it's hard knowing he's making these insane decisions."

"Look who's talking, I had the same conversation with Mommy about you years ago."

"And look what happened," I said.

"But you're thinking clear now right?"

"Yes."

"So you'll be ok. God works in mysterious ways," she preached.

"God's a practical joker, Mimi."

We spoke a little while longer until my fifteen minutes ran out. I couldn't imagine being present in the world, dealing with Drew's antics in such a calm manner. God does work in mysterious ways because there's times when the confines of my prison cell has felt like a sanctuary from some of Drew's behaviors. He's made the difficulties that normally come with being in prison easy to deal with.

*

Drew didn't take my advice about saving his money and after a couple of months, out of nowhere, he was living back in Florida with his mother. Somehow they seemed to work out their differences again but I was skeptical to how long it would last. I admit I was relieved he was back in Florida because the added worry and stress he was causing my mother had me concerned for her health and well-being. My situation already served as a crushing blow to the amount of stress any parent should have to tolerate from their child.

I called Drew once he sent me his Florida number.

"Tell me what made you move back to Florida?" I asked after we greeted one another.

"Mom finally broke up with Anthony, so it's all good."

"You got a job?"

"No, I'm helping with my brothers and sister while mom's at work," he said.

"Just try keeping things respectful at her house please."

"I will, I got this as long as Anthony ain't here, there's never a problem," he explained.

"You have your Court date coming up," I reminded him.

"Yeah, Grams brought me a plane ticket."

"I still think the plea is a good deal," I suggested with hope that he would listen.

"I'm going to take it as long as the probation is transferred down here," he said.

"That won't be a problem, and I'm glad to hear you're making that decision. It's the right one."

"I figured you would be, Dad," he replied.

"Drew, when you're at the house, please tone down the flamboyant-ness around the girls for me," I asked again.

"God! It's just who I am," he cried.

"I know, Drew, but it can confuse the girls being so young."

"Yeah, whatever!" he spat.

Hearing the disappointment in his voice didn't alter my stance on what I expressed.

"Drew, you have to think about everyone, Grams included."

"And who's thinking about me and how I feel?" he retorted, surprising me with his valid point.

"Son, I'm not trying to purposely hurt you or get you upset. I just want to keep the peace."

"You don't have to worry, Dad," he promised.

Drew kept his word when he went to New York by spending most of his time in the voodoo room on Gram's computer. He took the plea deal, and it was an uneventful visit. It was good to hear, and I could tell that my mother was happy to see him.

Once back in Florida it was hard to catch up with him again, and with his 21st birthday quickly approaching, all I could do was hope and pray he'd make it through.

Drew was out of contact for a few months, but he survived his 21st birthday with no incident. I received a new cell phone number sent from him in a short e-mail message, telling me to call. The first thing that stood out was that the area code was from New York. *And why was this?* I wondered.

"Long time no speak stranger," I said.

"Hey Daddy, good to hear your voice," he replied.

"Drew, where you been at?" I asked.

"Doing me, here and there."

"Did you move back to New York?"

"Yeah, I'm in the Bronx now, moved a few weeks ago," he said.

"What happened with living with your mother?"

"She got back with Anthony, and the two of us just can't live together," he answered.

"Drew, I haven't heard from you in over three months."

"Dad, I've been busy with my life, and could you do me a favor by not telling Grams I'm in New York?"

"Why? What's wrong with her knowing?"

"Because, she'll just stress me out, I don't want to be bothered worrying about her."

Did he really just say that? I thought to myself.

He was the one making her a nervous wreck so I was glad he didn't want her to know he was back in New York.

"If that's what you want."

"It is, Dad, for now at least."

"You have a job?"

"Yeah, I'm a greeter at T.G.I.F."

"Where you living?"

"With a close girlfriend, for now," he answered.

I wondered if his reason for living in the city was because he'd decided to pursue his female impressionist career, but I didn't ask and really didn't want to know, plus he was sharing enough.

"I've been going to mad parties and clubs now that I'm 21," he explained.

"Yeah."

"Um-humm, coming home at 6:30 am is a normal thing for me because that's how I do it!" he declared.

"Well, don't party too much, and I hope you're taking care of yourself," I said.

"You can never party too much, Dad. Take care of myself how?" he asked.

"With protection, Drew," I muttered.

"Oh, of course, I'm just surprised to hear that from you."

"I've told you in the past, but it's not a topic I'm going to constantly bring up because you should know," I told him.

"Nah, you're right, Dad, and I do," he answered.

Drew was sounding more feminine than ever. There was definitely no type of restraint with speaking to me, sounding just like a chick with a deep voice. Once we got off the phone, I called my mother to give her an update, which was more like a warning.

"Drew's living in the Bronx, but he doesn't want you to know for now," I told her that night.

"Why not?" she asked.

"Because you stress him out!"

"Oh yeah?"

"Yeah, I was shocked to hear that, so when he does contact you, which I'm sure he will, act as if you're surprised."

"Sure Son."

"He has a place to stay and a job but he sounds more girlish than ever," I admitted.

"Thanks for the heads up, Ed."

"All right, Mom. Love you!"

Once again, I was at a loss with my concerns for Drew. He was partying like a rock star now that he turned 21, and my street intuition told me that he was back using drugs. Still there was nothing I could do, even if I wasn't in prison. I couldn't control what Drew did with his life because it was his life to live. I had tried my hardest to give him advice but he was not trying to hear what I was saying, especially while I was preaching from a federal penitentiary.

When I saw openly homosexual men in prison, I hated the fact that they reminded me of my son, but I felt empathy for them nonetheless. Since it was no secret that I was writing this book, a few of them requested to read it, and I had no problem letting them hoping that they could understand some of what their fathers went through.

The Universe continued to bring me cellmates that were personally dealing with the issue. Esco was the first of many.

"D" had a nephew that was gay and his brother was having a real hard time accepting it. I had cellmates whose daughters were lesbians, one whose younger brother liked women and men. The leader of one of the most violent gangs confided to me that his son recently told him that he was gay, and he then proudly pulled out a recent picture of the 2 of them in the visiting room from that past weekend. We both seemed to share this unspoken bond with an extra degree of respect for one another for having accepting our sons for who they are.

Through the difficulties and challenges that we shared when telling stories to one another about our experience of being a father of a gay child, -regardless of how extreme another's story may seem- I could always easily top it with any number of Drew's episodes, safely securing his crown as the gayest man on the planet.

Drew appeared to be making sure that he'd never lose that title, when two months later he showed up unexpectedly at my mother's house to visit for the weekend.

CHAPTER FORTY-TWO

The sound of light taps knocking on my mother's front door caught Maria's attention. Opening it she found Drew wearing blue skin tight jeans, thick black mascara and red lipstick, with a Michel Kors pocketbook hanging from one shoulder and a small book bag with double straps filled with clothes dangling from the other. Batting his eyelashes, leaning back smiling, he spread both arms wide for a hug as he shouted...

"Surprise!!"

Maria was shocked, stuttering as she spoke slightly confused, "DDD-Drew?"

"The one and only, but it's Draya now," he announced, walking into the living room, ushering in the trace of recently smoked Newport's mingled with the scent of Christian Dior perfume.

"I just came to spend a few days with my family. I've missed you and the girls," he excitedly expressed.

"It's good to see you Drew but..."

"It's Draya, I go by Draya now," he corrected.

"Ok, but I wish you would have called us first," she finished saying.

"Then it wouldn't have been a surprise, and I love surprises," batting his lashes, his wide eyes locking with Maria's stare.

Nia came rushing down the stairs at the sound of Drew's girlish voice, running towards his open arms, then slowing her momentum once noticing the difference in his appearance.

"There's the Princess!" he said crouching down with arms outstretched, pulling her close for a tight hug.

"Hi," she greeted, a little above a whisper.

"Hey Sweetheart, where's Grams?" he asked.

"She'll be home soon," Maria answered. "I thought you were her actually."

"Well, then another surprise is on the way, I can't wait until I see her," he said.

The unexpected visit came with plenty of suspicion, especially since the last pop-in ended with the police not far behind.

"How long have you been in New York?" Maria asked, although she already knew he was living in the Bronx.

"For a few months, living in the city, getting settled before letting anyone know," he answered placing his two bags on the living room couch, then walking into the kitchen and opening the refrigerator door as he continued.

"What's to drink in here? Any wine?"

"No," Maria answered following behind him.

"Of course not, you folks in the suburbs are too slow, that's why I need to be in the city."

"There's some orange juice," Maria suggested.

"I guess that will do for now. Maria when you coming to the city so I can show you how to party?" he asked grabbing the Tropicana container, spinning around, closing the door with a bump from his hip, then reaching in the upper cabinet for a glass.

Seven-year-old Nia was now standing at the entrance to the kitchen staring at her brother who was sipping the juice, leaving a thick lipstick mark on the edge of his glass when he placed it on the counter half finished, and locking eyes with her saying, "Look how much you've grown sweetheart!" as Nia slowly walked to the security of her mother's side.

"Drew, you look a lot different since the last time we saw you," Maria pointed out.

"It's Draya, please, and I'm embracing my true self and no longer recognize that name so please just address me as Draya," he demanded.

"Ok, if you say so," Maria answered with raised eyebrows and a slight shake of her head.

"I do say so," Drew replied.

"Hellooo," came the cheery voice of Grams announcing herself walking through the front door. Nia dashed from the safety of her mother's hip into the arms of her Grandmother.

"There's my princess!" she said lifting her up, smiling and placing a kiss on both cheeks.

"Drew's here," Nia quickly informed her.

"Oh yeah?" Grams said as Drew appeared sticking his head from around the corner of the kitchen.

"Surprise, Grams!!" he sang while walking towards her, arms open wide.

"Hey Drew, what a nice surprise, come give me a hug."

"It's Draya!" Maria shouted from the kitchen.

"What, honey?" Grams asked.

"Oh that's what I go by now, Grams, Princess Draya," Drew answered strutting over embracing her in a tight hug.

"I've missed you, Drew," she said returning the embrace, looking over his shoulder seeing Maria throwing up her hands with a defeated quizzical look.

"I'm just here for the weekend, Grams, because I missed you all so much," he explained.

"That's fine, Drew, but didn't we speak about you giving us a heads up?"

"I just wanted it to be a surprise because it's been so long." he replied.

"Good thing I planned on spending the weekend home, we'll have time to catch up."

The e-mail I received from Maria just read: "CALL HOME NOW 911!!!"

Numerous thoughts raced through my mind at what the emergency could be. Maria answered on the first ring.

"What's the 911 all about?" I asked without even saying hello.

"Princess Draya showed up to spend the weekend."

"What, who?" I asked confusion resonating in my voice after expecting to hear some horrible news.

"Your son!" she shouted.

"Drew's at the house?"

"Yes, looking like some hoochie mama, wearing pounds of makeup, insisting we call him Draya."

"Oh my God," I said leaning my head against the base of the phone booth.

"I'm ready to leave and take the girls to Rhode Island until he's gone," she barked.

"Calm down, Maria, no one's in danger, your overreacting"

"Eddie, you should have seen Nia's face when she first saw him, she didn't know what to think. Shit, when I first saw him I didn't know what to think either."

"I know it's difficult but that's her brother," I reasoned.

"Brother or sister you mean, who knows because I don't have the answer to explain this to my daughters."

"There's nothing to explain," I said.

"What! He's their brother prancing around like he's Tinker Bell. Alexa is twelve but Nia is only seven, Eddie" she shouted.

"I didn't mean it like that, Drew's who he is, some things just don't have a logical explanation, he's one of them."

"I'm not asking for logical, I'm looking for sane!"

"Ok, how about letting me talk to my mother."

"Hold on!" she spat.

Hearing the click clack of Maria's high heels descending each step in the receiver as she walked downstairs, I only had a second to get my thoughts together regarding the handling of what seemed to be the kick off -in Drew's mind- of his life as the star of his homosexual reality show.

"Hello Son," my mother answered sounding as if all was as normal as can be.

"You sound calm while Maria's at Def-Con 1," I said.

"You know she tends to overreact."

"More like you underreact, Ma. Don't allow Drew to come and just do what he wants," I said.

"I know, Ed, he's just staying until Monday," she replied sounding as if she had everything under control.

"He has a new look and new name, huh?"

"Yes, well, I'm just calling him Drew."

"Just showing up like that, I don't know what's going on but he can't stay there, Mom," I reiterated.

"I know, Ed."

"We have to think about the girls," I emphasized.

"You don't have to explain it. I already know," she said sounding slightly annoyed.

"Ok, then I'll call tomorrow."

"Don't you want to talk to Drew?" she asked.

"No, Ma, I'll speak to him after I had some time to pray!"

"Ok," she said with a laugh. "You do that and say one for me."

Hanging up the phone, I walked to my cell, throwing myself on the bed wondering what this 180-degree change in Drew's attitude was all about. Did he need money? Was he on the run from the law again? Was he in some type of danger? Why would he, all of a sudden, show up like that with no call, no e-mail to me, or nothing?

The fact that he was totally violating the stipulations set on him just coming to visit was one thing we were letting slide, but he was turning it up when I'd asked him to tone it down at the house around the girls.

It's only for the weekend, I thought, hopefully things will stay quiet and uneventful. As I laid down to go to sleep another thought crossed my mind, *who was I fooling? When has anything in Drew's life been that way?* Never that I could recall. So all I could do was prepare myself for the next few days with Drew at the house and what that may bring.

*

Dressed in a similar fashion as the day before, Drew sat out on the front porch smoking a Newport in the late afternoon, when he saw his childhood best friend Vinny, stepping outside his house greeting a group of friends in a black suburban truck that pulled into his driveway.

Drew's face lit up with a smile as he headed next door, excited after not seeing his friend in a few years.

"Hey Vinny!" he shouted in his girlish voice, drawing the 4 guys in the truck and Vinny's attention.

"Oh my, God," Vinny said under his breath.

"Who the fuck is that?" one of the guys in the truck asked.

"It's just my crazy ass neighbor," Vinny told them lowering his voice as Drew approached.

"What's up Vin-vin?" Drew said giving him a playful slap on his right shoulder.

"Nothing much, Drew."

"Vin-vin?" one of the guys in the truck snickered.

"What's up? Someone say something?" Drew quickly snapped.

"No sweetheart," said another voice from inside the truck.

"You'd be surprised at how sweet it is," Drew shot back, causing the others to laugh and joke whichever one dared to make the remark.

"So Vinny, what's been up?" Drew asked ignoring the guys in the truck.

"I said nothing," emphasizing a harsh tone.

"Well aren't we a little moody. I just wanted to come say hi."

"Ok, Drew, take it easy," Vinny said in a dismissive manner.

Drew stood staring at his childhood best friend with whom he shared countless days riding bikes, wrestling with in the pool, sleep overs, watching movies, telling stories and secrets, promising to stay best friends no matter what. He recognized that the promise was broken.

"I get it Vinny," Drew said turning around walking at first, but then hearing sounds of the laughs and jokes being made at his expense, he began to jog back into the house where his grandmother noticed tears streaming down his face causing his mascara to smear.

"What's the matter, honey?" she asked standing up from her loveseat walking towards him.

"Nothing, Grams, it's nothing," he said wiping his tears on the sleeve of his shirt.

Embracing him in a hug she rubbed his back reassuring that whatever it was would be all right.

"Tell me what's bothering you," she asked.

"I was just at Vinny's and he acted like an asshole towards me with his stupid friends," he said.

"What did he do?"

"He was just cold, treating me like a stranger," he sobbed.

"Well, you know as well as anyone that people change," she said while continuing to rub his back.

*

When I called that evening I could hear that Drew was still upset.

"Grams e-mailed me about the situation today with Vinny," I told him in a comforting tone.

"He's just a jerk, I'm over it," he said.

"Drew, you have to understand that you probably put him in an awkward position."

"How's that?" he defiantly asked.

"His childhood best friend who used to sleep over his house is now a flaming homosexual. Come on Son, you know that opens him up to all types of jokes and ridicule," I explained.

"I would never treat him the way he treated me," he replied.

"I know that, but you have to consider the position you put him in. I know you didn't intend it, and it sucks that you should have to think about it, but guys that age are young and immature."

"Yes, they did act like a bunch of children" he replied.

"Sorry you had to go through that," I said.

"Don't be, it's his loss," he said, clearly defensive.

"What made you change your mind about letting Grams know you're in New York?" I asked changing the subject.

"I just missed my family," he huffed.

"There's no problems we have to worry about right?" I questioned.

"No."

"When do you have to be back at work?"

"Don't worry, Dad, I'll be leaving Monday morning," he snapped.

What I thought was a subtle question drove him bringing it right to the point.

"Ok then just try to-

"Tone it down, yeah I know how concerned you are for your girls," he spat and the next thing I heard was him passing Maria the phone without giving me a chance to reply.

"Hello," she greeted.

"Hey Love," I said, "how you holding up?"

"Well, today Nia asked me what a transvestite is."

"She did? Why?"

"Why do you think? When the ice cream truck came down the block, Drew took her to get a snow cone."

"Yeah."

"You know he turns everything into a spectacle with the process of ordering, and after he did whatever it is that Drew does, she overheard the neighbors talking about him calling him a transvestite, and since they were talking about her brother, she was upset and crying."

"Is she all right?" I asked.

"She's fine now but these aren't the type of questions she should be asking at her age."

"He'll be leaving on Monday so just hold tight," I said.

"If he doesn't, I've already made plans to say at my girlfriend's until he leaves," she threatened knowing that the girls are the one thing helping to keep my mother grounded.

"That won't be necessary," I said.

"You don't know, he's your mother's grandson, too."

"Just trust me," I repeated.

"Trust you?" she said. "Yeah, right."

Over the years of being locked away, our marriage had been deteriorating, which was something I knew would happen and understood, chalking it up to the lifestyle I lived. However, the feelings of rejection that Drew faced were all too common a reality. The way he got off the phone showed he was perceiving me as another person against him.

Although Drew made great attempts at masking his disappointments and anger, it seemed that the way he dealt with his feeling of rejection was to throw what you feared the most in your face, not giving a fuck about who else it affected.

He did just that on the morning when he was set to leave.

CHAPTER FORTY-THREE

"Drew, come on, honey, we're going to be late for your train," my mother called to the upstairs bathroom, early Monday morning.

The door swung open and out he stepped wearing an undersized pair of blue Daisy Dukes, a yellow halter-top exposing his stomach, accenting the piercing in his belly button, a bright red pocketbook and black 9" red bottom heels. He pranced down the stairs swinging his hips, smacking on his gum not trying to hear anything or say anything to anyone. He walked out the front door and into my mother's white Infinity, making his grand departure. Grams stood momentarily stuck at the disturbing sight of her grandson, holding her tongue until she got him alone in the car.

"Where in the world are you going dressed like that?" she asked starting the car for the drive to the Smithtown train station.

"Dressed like what Grams?"

"Like a prostitute, Drew!"

"It's Draya! And this is how I always dress," he answered back.

"And you wonder why people treat you so harshly, that's the most distasteful outfit I've ever seen and I wish you would change in the back seat."

"I'm not changing, this is the style," he said.

"I might be old but there's nothing stylish about that," she yelled.

"Whatever!!"Drew yelled back.

Nothing was said between the two of them for the rest of the ride to the Smithtown train station parking lot.

"I'm just glad the girls already left for school and didn't see this distasteful display," my mother said.

"The girls, the girls, that's all anyone cares about. What about me, Grams?" he shouted as he grabbed his bags, got out the car slamming the door.

She didn't chase after him. She calmly sat in the car, watching as he stood on the platform until a train pulled up heading east, the opposite direction of the city, but Drew got on it anyway. Pulling out of the parking lot with tears blurring her vision, it wasn't long until she was forced to pull over to the side of the road, wiping her eyes, crying her heart out for her grandson.

When I called, she explained her morning.

"He has no regard for anyone, which shows he doesn't care about himself, Mom."

"I know, Ed, but he's so young and vulnerable," she explained.

"But my girls are even younger, and I'm going to limit the effect that craziness Jennifer created in Drew on them," I said.

"It's not his fault, we should have done more," she whispered barely enough for me to hear.

"We did what we thought was best at the time, Mom."

"He didn't even head to the city," she said.

"Wherever he's going is up to him, as long as he's not at the house acting like that," I told her.

After hanging up the phone, I breathed a sigh of relief that Drew left. After hearing how he was dressed, and the behavior he displayed, another few months with one of his missing in action missions would be welcomed.

However, the very next morning the telephone rang.

"Grams, can you please pick me up from the train station?" Drew asked.

"Give me a few minutes to get dressed and I'll be there," she said with no hesitation.

Picking him up, she shook her head when seeing that he was dressed in the same attire as the day before. She didn't question where he spent the night. She stayed silent as he sat in the passenger seat explaining how he lost his money the night before. Listening she didn't drive back to the house, instead pulling into a nearby park on Maple Avenue to talk.

"Drew," she said after turning off the engine and unbuckling her seat belt, shifting her body to face him directly. "The behavior you've been displaying with no regards for anyone else has forced me to make the tough decision of no longer allowing you at the house unless you're prepared to adhere to our rules."

"So you're turning on me too?" he shouted.

"You think I want this Drew?"

"You're the one that's saying it," he barked.

"Because of your actions," she retorted.

"Is this the bitch Maria's work or my punk ass father's?" he asked.

"Maria has nothing to do with it. Your father and I discussed it, and we agree it's what's best for everyone," she explained.

"How is it best for me!" he shouted.

"Hopefully you'll realize how your actions affect others, and I hope you get the professional help you need."

"Fuck that, Grams, I hate you and my father. Take me back to the train station," he demanded.

It was a silent drive back to the station. As soon as my mother pulled into the parking space, Drew turned towards her, "Grams! You don't ever have to worry about seeing me again!" he shouted. Stepping out of the car, he slammed the door and stomped to the stairs leading up to the train platform.

Hearing my mother describe what occurred, I could tell she was extremely upset. I was supposed to be the one to tell Drew that he couldn't come to the house in that manner. But my mother took that burden, being blamed by Drew, causing her to feel overwhelmed with guilt.

"You should have let me tell him he can't come to the house," I said.

"Well, I didn't want to bring him to the house and have to wait for you to call, causing a scene in front of the girls," she explained.

"I understand, but you should have told him it was all me because it was, Ma," I said.

"That's not what's important, it's done, but he really needs help because something is very wrong."

"He has to want to help himself," I said.

"I know," she quietly replied.

"I'm going to call him and let him know that I said he can't come to the house dressing and acting anyway he wants."

"Don't be hard on him, Ed, he's sensitive," she said continuing, "He was upset and you don't know what else is going on in his life that has him acting out like that."

"I won't be Mom, don't worry."

*

There was no way for this to not be a hostile conversation. Drew already had a rough weekend being rejected by his childhood best friend, and arguing with my mother. Now I was about to call letting him knew he was no longer welcome at the house until he got some type of counseling, which I know he won't be receptive too. I'd be perceived as the bad guy. It tore at my heart to make this call especially since he's so fucking sensitive and erratic that I just didn't know what he'd do. These are the type of things that trigger suicide attempts and drug binges that lead to overdoses due to feeling alone and confused. But I couldn't continue to allow the type of insanity that he displayed, stress my mother to death and affect my girls in who knows what type of way. I think I'd have a panic attack if I called home and Nia told me her favorite color is blue. That though alone motivated me to head towards the phone because this call had to be made. "Drew."

"What Dad!" he answered in a turbulent tone.

"Grams, told me you left upset."

"Because everyone is against me," he answered.

"We're not against you Son, it doesn't make us happy to have to make these choices."

"Grams called me a prostitute!" he shouted.

"Because of the way you were dressed," I said.

"Don't we live in America? I'm free to dress any way I want," he replied.

"You're right, but we're also free to choose what we want to expose the girls to," I answered.

"Yes, the precious girls!" he spat.

"It's not only that Drew. You're, living on the wild side with all your partying and drinking" I explained.

"There's nothing wrong with that!" he defended.

No matter what I said he wasn't trying to hear it, but I still attempted to reason with the unreasonable.

"The fact that you can't see that there's something wrong with your behavior and the way you're dressing is proof that there's something wrong, Drew."

"Call me Draya! And if my strong personality and appearance disturbs you so much now, then you better prepare yourself and the family because I've been taking hormone pills and in 6 months I'll have the real body of a woman!" he defiantly spat.

Any psychodynamic perspectives I've attempted to apply explaining Drew's extreme mental distortions were just confirmed. Gripping the phone at a loss for words, I felt dizzy at what I heard.

"Did you hear what I said?" Drew's voice asked breaking the silence.

"Yes, I heard you," was all I could muster to say.

"Well?" he yelled wanting my reply.

"I don't think changing into a girl is going to make you happy."

"I disagree, it's the only way I will be happy," he answered back.

"You're still very young, Drew. Happiness must first be found within."

"Well, within I'm a woman, always have been, always will be, and in six months, Draya is all you'll see! I'm walking into work so I have to go."

Click.

I stood holding the phone to my ear a good 30 seconds after Drew hung up on me, stuck in a daze still. *Come on Mr. non-judgmental, unconditional love...snap out of it!* I thought to myself. Still I was trapped in a fog. The only voice of reason I thought could get through to Drew was Jennifer, so I went to the computer and e-mailed her a message in the hopes that she would reach out to Drew somehow.

I explained Drew's past few days on Long Island, the strict limitations on him coming to the house out of concerns for my other children, and of course this new revelation which I was sure she already knew about. I ended by letting her know that as a sign of respect, because she's his mother and the only person I thought he would listen to, I was asking for her help. I anticipated either silence or a complete deranged reply stating what a terrible father I've been and how I only care about my girls.

My facial expression must have revealed that I was stressed because my friend Twin followed me in my cell asking, "What's wrong with you?"

"I just got off the phone with Drew."

"He's still wilding out?"

Twin has grown to be one of my closest friends through the years, and I've often vented my frustrations with the situations I've dealt with concerning Drew to him.

"He's taking things to the next level!" I said.

"How? Wait, does he want you to meet his boyfriend?" he asked in all seriousness.

"No, that's one thing I've been preparing myself for. Drew's started taking hormone pills to turn into a woman," I confessed, shaking my head in disbelief.

"Get the fuck out of here!" he shouted with a surprised look on his face.

"Yeah, he just told me, and I tried to talk some sense to him but he's too upset to listen."

"You see that's why I'm not having any kids; all this shit you go through. I could never deal with that," he admitted pacing back and forth in the cell, then asking, "What are you going to do?"

"There's not much I can do. I e-mailed Jennifer about it, so I'll see what she says and take it from there," leaning back on my pillow stretching out on my bed.

"You think she already knows?"

"Yes."

"Without mentioning it to you?" he asked with a shocked expression.

"Why would she?"

"You're his father, that's why?"

"Only when it's convenient for her, plus I'm not expecting a rational response."

"So why e-mail her," he questioned.

"Because she's his mother and creation."

*

An hour later, I logged on to the computer and saw that Jennifer responded to my message. Preparing myself for a certain degree of lunacy, I took a deep breath and counted to 5 before clicking on her name.

To my surprise, the message began with Jennifer agreeing with everything that I explained to her in the message I sent. She told me that she already knew about Drew taking hormone pills and that she told him she wasn't in favor of it. She also agreed with what I expressed about him being too young to make such a drastic decision and thanked me for letting her know what was going on in New York as she hasn't heard from him in a few weeks.

Jennifer was agreeing with everything I said. *Could this really be happening?* I thought to myself. *Did she finally begin to see things from a sane perspective? Did I get myself all worked up for nothing, thinking she would say something crazy, blaming me for whatever came to her mind.* Just as I began to believe that, I read her last line:

By the way, I think you should know that Drew is H.I.V. Positive. Take care, Jennifer.

CHAPTER FORTY-FOUR

People often describe the way they would react when receiving disastrous news -Smashing anything in reach like the computer screen, punching the first person that gives the slightest attitude, shouting from frustration or just breaking down in tears overwhelmed from emotional pain.

Staring at the monitor, reading the last line continuously, all the noise in the common area went silent as if God hit the pause button on my life, leaving me stuck scrutinizing the words: H.I.V. Positive.

This wasn't one of Drew's crazy outlandish behaviors that I could laugh at to keep from crying, this was a grave matter. Mechanically, I logged off the computer, walking zombie-like into my cell. I grabbed my gray wool scarf hanging it over the door to block the glass for privacy. Lying back on my bed, I clearly pictured a six-month-old Drew sleeping on my chest, smelling the scent of milk on his breath from the empty baby bottle I prepared and feed him for his afternoon nap.

I clenched my eyes closed tight to keep me in that imaginary moment in time, fearing having to face the reality of the news I just received. I don't know how much time passed until the jingling of the C.O.'s key's making his rounds, coming closer to my cell, forced me back to the present. He tapped on my door since the glass was covered.

"I'm good!" I shouted, the standard reply they like to hear to insure I wasn't inside attempting to kill myself.

But, I wasn't good, I was devastated. My heart felt like it was trapped between a tightening vice grip, causing sharp pains running down the left side of my body. The air was hard to breath, perspiration building under my armpits, on top of my nose and head as I told myself.

Breathe deep, Eddie realizing my troubling thoughts were causing a physical effect.

Inhale.

1, 2, 3, I mentally counted,

exhale 3,2,1.

By repeating this meditation exercise 3 times, it helped me to relax offsetting the oncoming panic attack I almost caused myself.

The news of my father's death, even being sentenced to 45 years, none of those things impacted me the way reading this news did. H.I.V. Positive. The words flashed in my mind's eye. After another 30 minutes, I opened my door and walked to the phone.

"Hello Mom."

"Hey Son," she answered in her perky, lively voice.

I didn't know how to tell her over the phone. I thought about waiting for a visit but quickly ruled that out.

"I got some shocking news from Jennifer today concerning Drew."

"What happened? Is he all right?" she asked with worry and concern in her voice.

"No Ma."

"Oh my God, what is it?"

"My son is H.I.V. positive," I said tears trickling down my face as if speaking it out loud finally made it real. Expecting to hear a heart retching scream, some cry of agony or despair, she seemed unruffled which helped me to regain my composure.

"Well," she said, "two years ago I noticed a lump on his neck that caused me grave concern, and I pushed him to go get tested."

"You've known for two years, Mom!"

"No! I suspected it, he just told me he was positive during our argument at the train station. I was going to tell you when I came to visit this weekend."

"Jennifer beat you to that," I said.

"I guess she did. How you holding up?"

"I'm all right. Of course, upset but it's a little surreal to me."

"Being H.I.V. positive isn't the death sentence it used to be, Ed. Drew can live a productive life if he chooses to."

"Yeah, but it doesn't seem like that's the path he's on," I pointed out.

"I know, but hopefully that will change," she said. Having worked for the Suffolk County Health Department for over 30 years, specifically dealing with H.I.V., my mother was well informed, and she spent the remainder of the call telling me about all the new therapies they have and achievements that have been made over the years, assuring me they will find a cure in the near future. Her optimistic attitude was appreciated but my concern was whether or not Drew would make it to that near future.

We both agreed that the quality of his life would be based on his choice to be responsible with taking his medication and other important life changes. After the phone call, I logged back onto the computer, sending Jennifer a response to her message, asking her how long she's known, and was anything being done to help him deal with this. Her response informed me she's known about his health condition for 6 months. He has a regular medical doctor, nutritionist and psychiatrist that he sees. She also informed me that she does ask Drew if he's taking his meds, but feels like he brushes her off the way he answers, so she's done stressing about it since he wasn't worried about taking care of himself.

I didn't respond, I just logged off the computer once I read her message.

Walking back towards my cell, Twin was headed in my direction so I left my cell door open as he followed me in a few feet behind. Pulling back my chair, nodding my head offering for him to take a seat, I sat on my bed just shaking my head.

"What?" Twin asked, but I didn't say anything.

Then he said, "The shit with Drew turning into a woman? It's crazy but there's nothing you can do 'Mr. Love your kid whether their gay or straight'."

"It's not that Twin, I don't care that he's gay. I've been over that for years," I said.

"I know but being gay is one thing, actually turning into a woman is another!"

"Right now can you believe that even that is the least of my worries." I told him.

"No, I can't because I've seen you with your Guru attitude. All this 'allow life to unfold because things always work themselves out,' but honestly, Drew turning into a girl is fucked up! Your philosophy ain't working!" he said.

"It does appear that way, huh?" I answered.

"Don't hit me with your, things are rarely what they appear to be Mantra. That shit is for the birds!" Twin had himself all worked up sounding more upset than I was which was helping to calm me down.

"That's really not what it is Twin."

"Eddie, you're one of my best friends, how much worse could it be?"

"A lot."

"How?" he asked.

"Drew's H.I.V. positive."

"What!!" he shouted, eyes wide, nearly popping out of his face like one of those childhood cartoon characters. Letting his head drop, looking to the floor, we just embraced the silence for a few seconds until Twin stood up and said, "Come here Ed, you need a hug."

CHAPTER FORTY-FIVE

Reaching Drew took me a few days after constantly calling and getting his voice mail. Expecting the same and preparing to hang up, I was surprised to hear him press the number five accepting my call.

"Hellooo," he sang with a normalcy in his voice that caught me off guard since he didn't know I already knew about his condition, making me realize how strong and brave he was.

"How you doing, Son?"

"I'm fine, all is good. Just doing me," he answered.

"I've been trying to call you all week."

"Yeah, I saw the missed calls, I've just been busy."

"Well, I e-mailed your mother about your taking the hormone pills," I told him.

"She don't have anything to say to how I live my life. No one does!" he barked.

"You're right, I know but I had to reach out to somebody because that news fucked my head up," I admitted.

"You'll get over it," he quickly snapped.

"Drew!"

"What?" he asked clearly annoyed.

"Your mother told me about your health situation."

"Oh," he quietly said somewhat surprised.

"Why didn't you tell me yourself?"

"I don't know. I just wasn't ready for that."

"But you were ready to tell me you want to turn into a woman?"

"That's different," he replied.

"It's different but it's related Drew because they both have to do with your body," I said then continued, "right now you need to focus on being as healthy as you can be."

"I am," he shouted.

"Okay, but I don't think it's a good idea for you to start taking hormone pills along with the H.I.V. medication."

"Well, I've discussed it with my doctor and he said it's fine," spoken in an extremely defiant tone.

"Just because they're doctors don't mean they know everything, Drew."

"And you do?"

"Yes!" I said followed with a little chuckle in an attempt to lighten the pent up hostility.

"I've been taking both and I feel fine," he said.

"I'm really sorry to hear you in this situation, it's broken my heart," I admitted.

"It is what it is, I'll be fine." Drew tried to sound unconcerned but I knew he was scared. I was scared for him but I was also mad.

"How you deal with this is going to dictate the quality of your life."

"I know."

"All the drinking and drugs are going to take a toll on your body. You have to take care of yourself Drew."

"I always take care of myself," he stated.

"No, you haven't because I warned you about wearing protection, now look what happened."

"What happened was my cheating ass boyfriend!" he spat with anger and resentment spewing from every word.

"The only person to blame is yourself. You have to accept responsibility for your actions."

"Oh my God! I don't have time for this!"

Click.

The way that was handled was wrong. What I said was true but that wasn't the right time to say it. I definitely fumbled the ball and tried to call back to apologize but got no answer. I couldn't blame Drew for not wanting to tell me after what I just did and the full year long of silent treatment was a sign of just how much I hurt him.

Throughout that year I would hear second hand how he was doing from my sister or mother with the only message for me being, "He is still mad at me." I apologized and explained myself in numerous e-mails that went unanswered, still I sent a few messages each month just letting him know I still cared.

Drew had moved back to Florida a few months after we last spoke. A couple of months later he sent a message to me through Mimi, which read:

"Tell my father I've decided to stay a man."

Who would have ever thought that reading those words could bring such a huge smile to my face.

When Drew finally cooled off enough to send me his new cell phone number, I called right away.

"Hey old man!" he answered.

"So good to hear your voice, Son."

"Same here but I was mad at you."

"I know and I apologized in my messages."

"I read them but you know me, I like time to myself."

"How are you doing?" I asked.

"I'm good, living down here in paradise being a beach bum."

"Well, I'm still living in here being a convict," I joked.

"How's your book coming?" he asked.

"I had a little writer's block since you wouldn't answer my calls. Every time we talk it's a new chapter."

"I can give you a whole series of book to write," he said.

"Nah, that's all right, Drew, this one's been more than enough."

He sounded healthy and wasn't all over the map with the conversation. Although he still sounded like a girl (with my deep voice), there was no anger or resentment in what he said. Taking a more holistic perspective on life -eating right, taking his meds, practicing meditation, cross fit training and going to school to be a hairstylist (of course)- my son seemed to have his life on track.

Soon after Drew moved to Florida He took on the responsibility of helping to raise Alexis with his Grandmother Julie once Jennifer moved back to North Carolina. Something I was extremely proud to hear. But even if Drew wasn't doing all these positive things with his life, he was still my son.

*

It took an immense amount of development and growth on my part to attain this clarity of what being a father is. Looking back on my inner process, I'm able to recognize the corresponding circumstances that helped in my development. Growing up as a bi-racial child in the 70s, living in a single parent home in an all-white community, I learned what it felt like to be treated differently and the pain that's caused by other's ignorance.

The time spent in prison enlightened me to just how wide spread homosexuality is, and I was able to ask questions, gaining a deep insight while still being unreceptive to the whole father of a gay son idea. Working in the entertainment business exposed me to gay men and lesbian women, living productive lives, many of whom became good friends.

The seriousness dealing with suicide, drug abuse, alcoholism and H.I.V. made Drew's homosexuality practically null and void in regards to our relationship.

The world is a reproduction of our individual concepts and beliefs. At times, they may have to be challenged. There's nothing wrong with a father that embraces his homosexual child. That unconditional love and acceptance doesn't necessarily happen overnight; it was a process that developed as I matured.

With all the obstacles we've confronted over the years, Drew and I continue to share an unbreakable bond which is appreciated by the both of us. Working my brain to come up with a snazzy enlightened line to get my message across in this writing isn't needed because it's a basic truth simply stated:

Fathers need to be Fathers.

The End.

Made in the USA
San Bernardino, CA
04 August 2016